little buddy

—chris seidman

little
buddy

what a rookie father
learned about God from
the birth of his son

New
Leaf
Books

Orange, California

LITTLE BUDDY
published by New Leaf Books

ISBN 0-9700836-3-7

Printed in the United States of America

For information:
New Leaf Books, 12542 S. Fairmont, Orange, CA 92869
1-877-634-6004 (toll free)

02 03 04 05 06 07   9 8 7 6 5 4 3 2

In memory of

Harry Seidman & Doug McKnight,

two fathers who were

recently relocated to eternity

with the Father in heaven.

CONTENTS

"As the nurses cleaned him up and took his vital signs I made my way slowly over to where he lay. He looked a bit lethargic, lying there with his eyes shut while the nurses did their thing.

The words flew out of my mouth before I knew it. "Hey, little buddy!" The moment I said those words he turned his head in my direction and his eyes shot open. I thought my heart was going to fly up my esophagus and out of my mouth."

Introduction

Mornings with Skyler

I love mornings with my son, Skyler. When he wakes up, one of the first words out of his mouth is "Da-a-ddy." In a milli-second, I'm barreling into his room with out-stretched arms. He's usually standing up in his toddler bed, with tussled hair and bleary eyes, ready to leap into my arms. The first thing he wants to do is look into the mirror on his wall. (This is brave. I'm not a pretty sight early in the morning. Of course, some of my friends would say I'm never a pretty sight, regardless of what time of day it is.) While I'm holding him, he points at the reflection of me in the mirror and says over and over, "Da-ddy...Da-ddy."

There is nothing unusual or extraordinary about this. This exchange between a parent and a small child happens every day all over the world. Why are we so enthralled with being called "daddy" or "mommy" in those early years of parenthood? Haven't you seen your share of parents teaching (or maybe badgering) their infants and toddlers to call them by name? "Can you say 'daddy?' Can you say 'mommy?' Say it...please say it!"

Prior to parenthood I thought this desire was some kind of parental ego trip. After my first year of fatherhood I realized that it was nothing but a love trip. To love someone is to long to be loved by that someone. From the initial moments of parenthood we long for our children to see us, know us, call us, and respond to us.

So it is with God and His children. God longs for us to see Him, know Him, call Him, and respond to Him. His heart beats for such things. It's significant that of the scores of names that belong to God in Scripture, Jesus instructs us to address God as our "Father" when we pray to Him (Matt. 6:9). While God is, no doubt, honored when we address Him as our King, Rock, Shelter, Refuge, Deliverer, Savior, Redeemer, Warrior or Friend, the name He longs for us to call Him is "Father." God reveals His desire for an intimate relationship by asking us to use such a term of endearment when we call upon Him.

A Glorious Father

The apostle Paul called God the "glorious Father" or the "Father of glory" (Eph. 1:17). The word "glory" is often used but seldom understood. What does it mean and how does it help us to understand what kind of Father God is?

My wife and I are different in many respects. But perhaps one of our most glaring differences appears when we change the diapers of our little ones. She is a waste management specialist, doing it with speed and efficiency while using a minimal number of wipes and leaving no residue. As for me, well, I am twice as slow, not nearly as efficient, use three times as many wipes, and sometimes make more of a mess than I had when I began.

Because I'm not very quick and Skyler is moving quicker, changing diapers has become a challenge. More than once he's managed to elude me in the midst of a diaper change and lead me on a wild goose chase throughout our house. If you are a parent you probably have chased a stark-naked toddler around while trying to strap on a diaper (on the toddler, not you). Inevitably, my wife or I will exclaim in response to his nakedness, "There he is! In all his glory!"

Why do we say that? Because, believe it or not, that's exactly what "glory" means. It is the visible presence of something that was once invisible. It is the revealed presence of something that was once concealed. To glorify something is to bring out into the open what is hidden. When the Bible speaks of the glory of God, it is speaking of the manifest presence of God.

When Paul attached the adjective "glorious" to the word "Father" he was acknowledging that God is the type of father who puts Himself in position to be seen, known, called upon and responded to. He doesn't hide from us or make it difficult for us to get to know Him. Isaiah 6:3 records the words of the seraphs hovering over and around the throne of God in the heavenly realms—"the whole earth is full of his glory!" The earth is indeed full of God's manifest presence. The Apostle Paul acknowledged this in Romans 1:20: "For since the creation of the world God's invisible qualities—his eternal power and divine nature—have been clearly seen, being understood from what has been made."

God has made it possible for us to come to know Him through the visible and tangible things of our world. Have you ever looked at a sunset and been reminded of who's really in charge of this world? Have you ever gawked at majestic mountain peaks and been jerked back into the reality of how much bigger God is than you and your problems? Have you ever shaken your head at the brilliant lines, patterns and colors on the wings of a butterfly and contemplated the stunningly detailed imagination of the Creator? Then you've seen God's glory and encountered the efforts of a Father longing to be recognized by His children.

The Extraordinary in the Ordinary

In her work "Aurora Leigh," Elizabeth Barrett Browning wrote:

> Earth's crammed with heaven,
> And every common bush afire with God;
> But only he who sees takes off his shoes;
> The rest sit round it and pluck blackberries.

Browning eloquently acknowledges a curiously common feature of how God has worked in the lives of human beings for thousands of years. He has wrapped Himself up in the clothing of the ordinary things, events and people of our everyday lives. His taking on human form in the person of Jesus Christ isn't the only example, it's just the ultimate one. Both before and since the carpenter from Nazareth walked the dusty roads of our planet, God has been engaged in the work of clothing the extraordinary in the ordinary and using the ordinary to teach us about the extraordinary.

He used a worm and a vine to get a message across to the cantankerous prophet Jonah. He used a linen belt and a visit to a potter's house to instruct Jeremiah. He even used a donkey, of all things, to speak some sense into Balaam. And who can forget how He got Moses' attention? It was through an ordinary thorn bush, set ablaze in the middle of a desert, that God called him.

A pagan once asked a rabbi why God chose to speak to Moses from a thorn bush. He thought that God would have spoken through the deafening sound of thunder and the blinding sight of lightning on the peak of some magnificent mountain. The rabbi answered, "To teach you that there is no place on earth where God's glory is not, not even in a humble thorn bush."[1] The ordinary things, events and people of our everyday lives often house the extraordinary and instruct us regarding the extraordinary. Such instruction never contradicts the revelation of Scripture but rather brings old truths into new light.

Browning was also aware that it's possible for us to miss the extraordinary in the midst of the ordinary. Many times we do not "see" and "take off our shoes." Instead, we "sit around and pluck blackberries." Paul wrote to the believers in Ephesus, "I keep asking that the God of our Lord Jesus Christ, the glorious Father, may give you the Spirit of wisdom and revelation, so that you may know him better. I pray also that the eyes of your heart may be enlightened…." (Eph. 1:17-18).

"That you would know him better"—this is the passion of a lover of God. It's in and through the ordinary that our extraordinary Father pursues us and interacts with us on a daily basis. For this reason, I frequently pray for the the eyes of my heart to be opened so that I can see the Extraordinary One through the ordinary things, events and people in my life.

The Rookie

When Tara first told me she was pregnant I was bombarded with a variety of feelings ranging from excitement, to apprehension, to sheer terror and, eventually, nausea. After going through the initial, and what I would later learn to be fairly normal, feelings of a rookie-to-be dad, I had the peculiar sense that I was about to be thrust into a learning curve. Of course I was going to find out "up close and personal" what happens to a woman's body, mind, and emotions when she becomes a home for another human being. But I also sensed that I was going to learn a great deal about myself in the coming months.

In the months preceding the birth of our firstborn, I made a deliberate effort to pray for God to give me a spirit of wisdom and revelation for the purpose of knowing him better through the first experiences of fatherhood. As wondrous and mysterious as childbirth and parenthood are, these experiences are nevertheless quite common. The last thing I wanted to do was leave my shoes on, sit around and pluck blackberries.

It doesn't really surprise me that God would use a baby as an instrument of instruction and revelation in my life. After all, the children that the disciples saw as a hindrance to Jesus became an instrument of teaching in His hands (Lk. 18:15-17). "I tell you the truth, anyone who will not receive the kingdom of God like a little child will never enter it." Jesus used children to teach adults a critical lesson about their spiritual lives. And He still does today.

In Scripture one of the most common metaphors describing the dynamics of the relationship between God and human beings is the relationship between a father and his children. It only makes sense that the initial experiences of fatherhood in my life would bring me fresh insights into old biblical truths about the heart of God. Through my rookie experiences of fatherhood I hope I can convey to you some of the wonder and mystery of our relationship with God.

What I'm going to share with you from my rookie experiences really isn't as much about my sons and me as it is about God and us. I've caught a glimpse of God's heart for me through my heart for my son, and I hope that you will catch a glimpse into God's heart for you as well. I'm well aware that my journey is just beginning.

Some of you are already far down the road of parent-hood and have important milestones in your rear view mirrors that I can't even see out of my front windshield right now. Perhaps I can serve to help you frame such experiences and milestones and give you a moment to "see," "take off your shoes" and consider what the Extraordinary has to say to you through the ordinary.

Others of you have yet to travel the road of parent-hood—or may never. The metaphor of parenthood should not deter you in the least from reading this book; in fact it can encourage you to keep your spiritual eyes open for the ordinary bushes that are set ablaze by God in your life. The old rabbi was right. There's no place on earth where God's glory is not. I invite you to visit the burning bush of rookie fatherhood with me. I hope that, together, we'll journey so deeply into the heart of God that we'll never find our way out.

Chapter 1

Broken to be Birthed

Prior to the birth of Skyler, Tara and I attended a parenting class for "rookie parents" at a local hospital. I must admit that I wasn't incredibly excited about having to miss Monday Night Football, but my fear of newborns far outweighed my love for football. You would be hard pressed to find someone more clueless than "yours truly" was when it came to babies. Though I tried not to have the look of a deer caught in the headlights, I'm sure it appeared that way every Monday night.

Every week was a learning experience, especially the week that we were shown a videotape of women giving birth. Following the videotape, I couldn't help but ask if men had the same access to the drugs available for their pregnant wives during labor and delivery. Well, you know the answer to that question. I just thought I'd ask.

One of the things I learned about labor and delivery was that in some cases a baby's frame would be of such size that his collar bones would naturally compress to the point of breaking as they passed through the birth tract. This didn't happen to Skyler, but it did to the baby boy of some very good friends of ours.

When I learned about this occasional occurrence I couldn't help but think how much this parallels our spiritual lives. The truth is that every one of us must first be broken in order to be birthed. This brokenness doesn't just happen once, but rather precedes every move to a new level of intimacy with God and use by God for His purposes in this world. God allows us to be broken down in order that He may build us up. God allows us to be bruised so that He can use us more fully. God allows us to be made weak enough in the knees so that we will fall to our knees—and in falling ultimately stand.

Isn't this one of the things the Apostle Paul was conveying in his second letter to the Corinthians? Consider these words: "We do not want you to be uninformed, brothers, about the hardships we suffered in the province of Asia. We were under great pressure, far beyond our ability to endure, so that we despaired even of life. Indeed, in our hearts we felt the sentence of death. But this happened that we might not rely on ourselves but on God, who raises the dead" (2 Cor. 1:8-9). Have you ever stood in Paul's sandals? Have you ever been under great pressure, far beyond your ability to endure? Has your heart ever felt like it was on Death Row? As Paul looks in the rear view mirror of his life he reflects on the reason he suffered adversity: "But this happened that we might not rely on ourselves but on God, who raises the dead."

Paul weaves this thought throughout his letter to the Corinthians and brings it to a climax in 2 Corinthians 12:9-10: "But he [the Lord] said to me, 'My grace is sufficient for you, for my power is made perfect in weakness.' Therefore I will boast all the more gladly about my weaknesses, so that Christ's power may rest on me. That is why, for Christ's sake, I delight in weaknesses, in insults, in hardships, in persecutions, in difficulties. For when I am weak, then I am strong."

The secular world would consider Paul to be "a few sandwiches short of a full picnic," if you know what I mean. Who would delight in weakness and in the realities of life that would drive us to such weakness? One who knows that after brokenness comes birth. One who knows that being broken precedes being birthed to a new level of intimacy with and empowerment by God.

It's to people who know and value this kind of intimacy, empowerment and maturity that James writes: "Consider it pure joy, my brothers, when you face trials of many kinds, because you know that the testing of your faith develops perseverance. Perseverance must finish its work so that you may be mature and complete, not lacking anything" (James 1:2-4). We can only consider such adversity "pure joy" if we value what it will do to form us into the image of Jesus Christ. Adversity is the furnace in which we are shaped and refined into his image. The degree to which we have "pure joy" is dictated by the degree to which we value growing in Christ.

There may be no plant on earth that inspires more awe than the giant sequoia tree. A few years ago I had the privilege of seeing these grand old trees with my own eyes. Some of them are more than 2,500 years old. According to a recent article in *USA Today*, these trees are also proof of the old adage that wisdom comes with age.[2] Lately these trees have been playing a central role in the education of foresters and the revision of their thinking about a forest's worst enemy—fire. Foresters and scientists are now trying to help people understand that natural forest fires, caused by lightning strikes for example, play a critical role in the conception, formation and survival of the giant sequoia trees.

These fires accomplish three things. First, the fires actually create openings in forest canopies and underbrush thereby enabling sequoia seeds to thrive. Second, they burn away other plant species that compete with the sequoia for water. Finally, the intense heat from the fires forces the sequoia cones to open and drop additional seeds on the ground. There are blessings in the burnings when it comes to the formation of the giant sequoia trees.

Isn't this the case in our spiritual formation? Don't we find that sometimes those things that we consider blessings in our lives actually turn out to form a canopy that distracts us and overshadows our spiritual concerns? Jesus warned about this canopy of distraction and how it can choke the spiritual life out of us. "The seed that fell among thorns stands for those who hear, but as they go on their way they are choked by life's worries, riches, and pleasures, and they do not mature" (Lk. 8:14).

But then a fire is unleashed and such things are consumed, enabling the spiritual seeds in our lives to have exposure to the Son through a restored focus upon Him in the midst of our adversity. No longer are such things competing with our relationship with God, and the heat produced from the fires releases new seeds for spiritual growth into the soil of our lives. There are blessings for our lives in the burnings of our lives.

Someone once came upon Michelangelo chipping away with his chisel at a huge, shapeless piece of rock. He asked Michelangelo what he was doing and he responded, "I'm releasing the angel imprisoned in this marble." This is what has to happen for us to be spiritually birthed and released during the course of our lives. One of the most fantastic things about the sovereignty of God is that He can use the adversity that we, others or Satan (or a combination of all three) introduce into our lives. In His hands such adversity can be used as a chisel breaking us down in order to set us free and forming us into what He wants us to be.

What is sometimes true biologically is always true spiritually. We must be broken in order to be birthed.

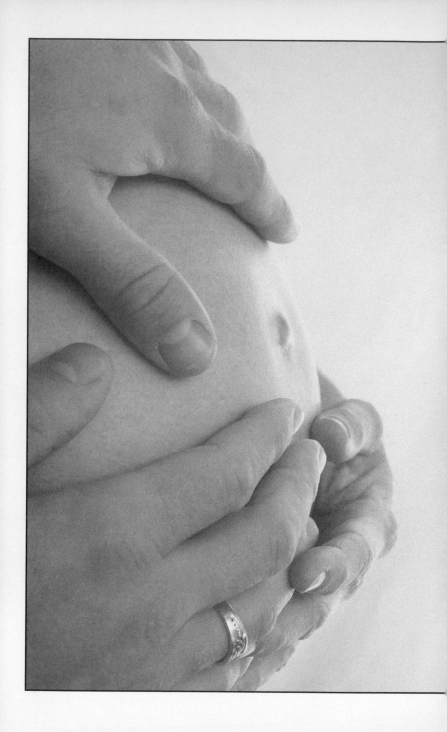

Chapter 2

Little Buddy

When Tara was pregnant with Skyler, I got more than my share of advice for what to do and expect as a rookie dad. I appreciated everyone's efforts—some, I would have to admit, more than others. One dad made some particularly strong recommendations regarding what one should never say to his pregnant wife:

"The baby is due the 25th! That's the date of the Super Bowl for cryin' out loud!"

"Did you eat all the ice cream again?"

"Have your ankles always looked that fat?"

"Look how fast Julie has recovered and gotten her body back after having that baby."

Or my personal favorite: "You're not going to pull that trigger."

Some of the most frequent advice I received from other fathers was to talk to my son while he was in the womb. Father after father relayed to me the marvel of their children recognizing their voice just moments after they entered the world. With this in mind I often carried on a conversation with, what amounted to, my wife's belly. When I would speak to him I would usually refer to him as my "little buddy" (no, it wasn't in memory of the Skipper and his relationship with Gilligan, but thanks for asking). "Little buddy, what's goin' on in there?" "Little buddy, when you gonna come out and see us?"

At first, I felt somewhat silly and, I suppose, even embarrassed. There was a part of me that was doing it just so I could satisfy all those fathers badgering me with their advice. But what happened the day my "little buddy" made his debut into our world suddenly helped me see that these one-sided conversations were more than worth the silly feelings of carrying on a conversation with my wife's belly.

Just moments after Skyler was born the nurse placed him on a warmer in the corner of the labor and delivery room. I had never been around a baby this "new." He had a cone-shaped head and the usual residue from the trip through and out of my wife's body. I must confess that Skyler looked a little worse-for-the-wear. It appeared that he had been on a fairly rough trip. The only pictures of newborns that I had ever seen were ones where the babies were clean, fresh and swaddled, as if they had come into the world in such a way.

As the nurses cleaned him up and took his vital signs I made my way slowly over to him. He looked a bit lethargic, lying there with his eyes shut while the nurses did their thing. The words flew out of my mouth before I knew it. "Hey, little buddy!" The moment I said those words he turned his head in my direction and his eyes shot open. I thought my heart was going fly up my esophagus and out of my mouth. It was only a few seconds later that a thought straight from the Spirit of God and attested to in Scripture shot across my mind. "This must be how the Father feels when His children hear His voice and turn in His direction!"

Through this initial experience of rookie fatherhood I was granted a glimpse of the heart that God has for His children. He longs for us to look in His direction. In those first months with Skyler, I would come home from the office and immediately get down on my hands and knees, crawling over to him in the living room. He'd be flat on his back or on his side playing with a simple toy. Most of the time he was completely oblivious to my efforts to get his attention. All I wanted him to do was look me in the eye and register a look of love, affection or acceptance. It was as though I was living for my son to look in my direction. It got to the point that I didn't even notice whether other adults were in the room when I came home. I wasn't really concerned about how foolish or silly I appeared in their eyes. After kissing Tara, I was immediately flat on my belly trying to get my boy's attention.

This is how God feels about you. As much as you long to be unconditionally loved and accepted by others and Him, do you know that He longs to be unconditionally loved and accepted by you? He longs for you to look in His direction. Scripture makes it clear that He is One who will "crawl on all-fours" and enter into our world at "eye-level" in order to get our attention.

Consider what Paul says about God to the people of Athens: "The God who made the world and everything in it is the Lord of heaven and earth and does not live in temples built by hands. And he is not served by human hands, as if he needed anything, because he himself gives all men life and breath and everything else. From one man he made every nation of men, that they should inhabit the whole earth; and he determined the times set for them and the exact places where they should live. God did this so that men would seek him and perhaps reach out for him and find him, though he is not far from each one of us" (Acts 17:24-27).

Most people think that Christianity is all about us seeking God when the truth is that it's more about God seeking us. He works through events in our lives in order to put Himself in position for us to seek Him, reach out for Him, and find Him. He is in white-hot, zealous, passionate pursuit of a relationship with each one of us.

What makes this so incredible is that God doesn't need us. Paul made this clear when he said that God wasn't "served by human hands as if he needed anything." Indeed, God is secure and well-established. He can live without us. But this truth serves to highlight His love for us all the more. God pursues us because He wants a relationship with us and not because He "needs" us. Just as I could live without Skyler so He can live without us, and just as I don't want to live without Skyler so God doesn't want to live without us.

Our Father God so longs for us to look in His direction that He's been shameless in His efforts to get our attention. He sent His Son to die on a cross to explain His love for us in a language we could understand. John put it this way in I John 3:1,16: "How great is the love the Father has lavished on us, that we should be called children of God! And that is what we are! ...This is how we know what love is: Jesus Christ laid down his life for us." Scripture is a love story about God going to great ends to get the attention of His people. And that love story continues today.

Have you seen Him lately trying to get your attention? Have you heard Him? He longs for you to look in His direction. Isn't it time you did?

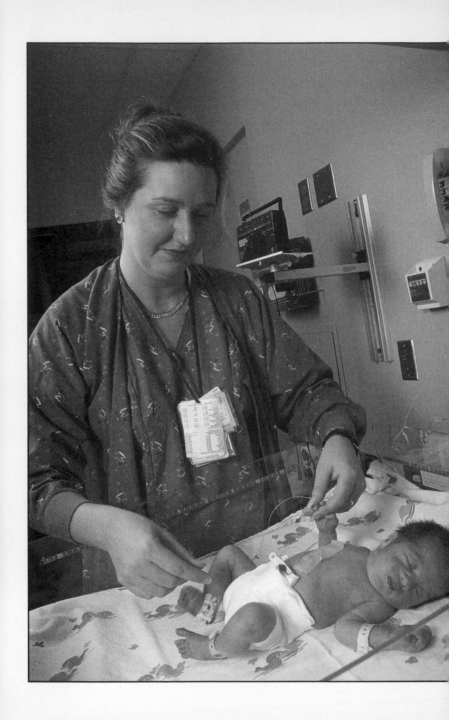

Chapter 3

Lone Ranger Christianity

The day before Skyler was born another little boy named Caleb made his way into the world, albeit fairly early—15 weeks early to be exact. Rex and Cathy were friends of ours who lived in Panama City which is about two hours drive from Pensacola. Due to a fragile pregnancy and some sudden and serious complications, Cathy was taken to a children's hospital in Pensacola designed for welcoming premature babies into the world and nurturing them.

In many ways our experience greatly differed from Rex and Cathy's. Not only were we in different hospitals, but the labor/delivery experience and the months thereafter proved to be filled with far less stress and uncertainties than what Rex and Cathy had to face.

I'll never forget walking into that special section of the hospital exclusively designed for premature babies. My baby seemed liked a giant as I gazed at the fragile little body of Caleb—all one pound and fourteen ounces of him hooked up to a variety of tubes doing everything from monitoring his vital signs to giving him nourishment. He could fit in the palm of my hand. There were entire rows of premature babies in this particular wing of the hospital.

It's difficult to describe the sensations one experiences in such a place. There was a thick spirit of apprehension, fear and anxiety on the part of the parents ever-hovering over their children. This was quite understandable when you take into account the fragility of life, and how acutely aware everyone in the room was of it. But a peculiar sense of hope and expectancy was also present. It was as though the wonder of new life would not allow itself to be overshadowed by threats to that new life. I don't entirely know why, but it's in these places that I sense the presence of angels more strongly than anywhere else.

If you've ever been around a baby born prematurely, you have seen for yourself why it's so important for her to remain in the mother's womb for the full term. There's no place more suited for the formation of a human being than a woman's womb. What is true biologically is also true spiritually. There's no place more suited for the formation of a spiritual being than in a body—a body of believers. I've been told time and time again by people who belong to the church family at "5th and Bedpost" that one can be a Christian without being a part of a church body. I don't spend time debating that issue. What I do know is that it's impossible to grow as a Christian without being part of a local body of believers.

Growing spiritually is tough any way you slice it. It may be difficult enough to grow spiritually in a church family, but it's impossible without it. Maybe this is why the writer of Hebrews said to a community of believers, "But encourage one another daily, as long as it is called Today, so that none of you may be hardened by sin's deceitfulness" (Heb. 3:13). He added, "And let us consider how we may spur one another on toward love and good deeds. Let us not give up the habit of meeting together, as some are in the habit of doing, but let us encourage one another" (Heb. 10:24-25). The Hebrew writer makes it clear that being a part of a body of believers has everything to do with not being hardened by sin's deceitfulness and staying spiritually pliable in God's hands as He shapes us into Christ's image.

When I think of the life of Christ being nurtured inside of us, I can't help but think of the beautiful story of the interaction between Mary, the mother of Jesus, and Elizabeth, the mother of John the Baptist (Lk. 1:26-45). While this story is about two women carrying children, it has much to say to all of us who carry Christ within us. God wants to do the same extraordinary act in our lives that He did in Mary's life—conceive and grow Christ within us. This is why I believe that we can glean some principles for Christ-carrying in our daily lives from Mary's story. And we'll find as we journey through life that the miracle of Christ living inside of us is no less extraordinary than Mary's.

Mary had her challenges, that's for sure. She was a rural Jewish virgin (most likely a teenager) who was engaged to be married. The angel Gabriel visited her and informed her that God had chosen her to be the mother of His Son. Can you imagine what might have been running through Mary's mind? "I'm still a virgin, but God is going to conceive His Son within me! How in the world am I going to explain this to Joseph?" If you were Joseph what would you think?

After we had decided to get engaged, my wife Tara and I spent a summer apart. I had an internship with a church in Amarillo and she worked as a receptionist in Fort Worth. Suppose she had come to me at the end of that summer and said, "Chris, I have to tell you something and I know it's going to be difficult for you to believe. Are you ready? Okay, I'm pregnant, but I'm still a virgin and God's the Father." Sure, honey, whatever you say, and I look forward to winning my first Grammy next year!

Do you see how ridiculously wondrous is the whole story surrounding the birth of Christ? We have no record of her trying to explain it to Joseph, but she must have tried because Matthew 1:19 says that when Joseph learned of her pregnancy he made up his mind to divorce her—which was what one did in Jewish culture in order to break an engagement. It took the angel of the Lord appearing to him in a dream to convince Joseph to change his mind and take Mary to be his wife (Matt. 1:20). Until the dream it was apparent that Joseph didn't believe her. Can you blame him?

Upon finding out she was pregnant with the Son of God, Mary knew she had a challenging road ahead of her. Perhaps this is why she "hurries" (Lk. 1:39) some 70 miles south of Nazareth to the hill country of Judea to see her relative Elizabeth and ends up staying with her for three months. I'm not sure whether she went to see Elizabeth before she told Joseph, fearing what he would say, or after she told him and was told, in return, that the wedding was "off." What I do know is that Mary needed Elizabeth's ministry.

Elizabeth and Mary didn't have much in common other than being blood relatives. Elizabeth was elderly, barren and the wife of a priest. They lived 70 miles apart which was quite a distance in a time when you were fortunate to get a donkey as your vehicle. But what drove Mary to make that 70 mile journey across rugged terrain, and what drew these two women from diverse backgrounds together, was the common ground of participating in an extraordinary plan of God.

Elizabeth understood what it was to be on the receiving end of a miraculous impartation of God. Luke introduces her as an elderly woman who had been unable to have children and yet Luke's drama begins with God seeing to it that she gets pregnant in her elderly, barren condition. God had called her to be the mother of John the Baptist who would prepare the way for Jesus.

If there was anybody who would believe and understand Mary's story, it would be Elizabeth. The moment Mary walked through the door and greeted Elizabeth, the baby inside of Elizabeth leaped. Elizabeth, filled with the Holy Spirit, said in a loud voice, "Blessed are you among women, and blessed is the child you will bear! But why am I so favored that the mother of my Lord should come to me? As soon as the sound of your greeting reached my ears, the baby in my womb leaped for joy. Blessed is she who has believed that what the Lord has said to her will be accomplished" (Lk. 1:42-45).

It must have been music to the ears of an excited—yet lonely and frightened—teenage girl who was looking for someone to believe in her, support her and encourage her. Did you notice how Elizabeth encouraged Mary? First she tells Mary how blessed she is to be chosen to be the mother of Jesus (vs. 42), and then she tells Mary how blessed she will be for believing that what the Lord had said to her would be accomplished (vs. 45). Elizabeth shows us two ways to encourage others who are facing the day-to-day realities of carrying Christ within them. We remind them of how special they are to God, then we affirm them for their faith in God. It's not hard to figure out why Mary stayed with Elizabeth for three months.

Charles Plumb was a jet fighter pilot in Vietnam. After some 75 combat missions, his plane was destroyed by a surface-to-air missile. He lived to tell about it.

One day, years later, Plumb and his wife were sitting at a restaurant while on vacation. A man walked up to their table and said, "You're Plumb, aren't you? You flew jet fighters in Vietnam from the aircraft carrier Kitty Hawk. You were shot down!"

Startled, Plumb asked in reply, "How in the world did you know that?" The man said that he had packed Plumb's parachute. Plumb gasped in surprise and gratitude while the man shook his hand and said, "I guess it worked."

It certainly did. If it hadn't, Plumb wouldn't have been there in that restaurant. He couldn't sleep that night thinking about that man. He kept wondering what the packer might have looked like in his Navy uniform. He thought about how many times he might have passed him on the Kitty Hawk. He wondered how many times he might have seen him and not even said, "Good morning." He pondered how many hours the sailor had spent in the parachute loft carefully weaving the shrouds and folding the silks of each chute. For the first time in his life Plumb was considering the importance of the person who had packed his parachute.

What that sailor did for fighter pilot Charles Plumb is what Elizabeth did for Mary. She packed her parachute. Believers tend to hold Mary in high regard for being the woman who carried Jesus in her womb. But don't forget Elizabeth who was there to affirm and support Mary at a critical moment—when she had come face-to-face with the exciting, challenging, lonely reality of carrying Christ within her.

Every Christ-carrier needs someone to pack their parachute. As extraordinary a blessing as it is to carry Christ inside of us, it can be, nevertheless, fearful and lonely at times. Like Mary we all know what it is to have people in our lives who don't believe or understand that God is at work in our lives bringing about the life of His Son within us. We all have people in our lives who don't understand, respect or encourage our submission to God's plan for Christ to grow within us. As in Mary's case with Joseph, sometimes these people are ones that we love dearly and are closest to yet who understand us the least.

You can do no greater thing with your life than submit to God's passion and plan for Christ to be formed in you. That's why we all need an Elizabeth. As Christ-carriers we all need someone to pack our parachutes— someone to provide what we need to get through life as Christ-carriers. Perhaps this is one of the reasons why the angel Gabriel mentioned to Mary (Lk. 1:36) that she wasn't the only one on the receiving end of a miraculous pregnancy. Perhaps the angel's words were not just to assure her that if God could make an elderly barren woman pregnant then He could make the virgin Mary pregnant. Maybe they were also to assure her that somebody else would accompany her on this extraordinary journey.

God doesn't expect or want you to be the Lone Ranger when it comes to your relationship with Him. This, among other reasons, is why He has seen fit to call us all into a local body of believers. The Christian life is more than just a matter of believing. It's a matter of belonging. By belonging to a community of faith we put ourselves in position for our parachutes to be packed.

The Amazon River is the largest river in the world. The mouth of this great river is more than 90 miles wide, and so much fresh water comes flowing out of it that one can detect the Amazon's currents two hundred miles out in the Atlantic Ocean. One of the ironic realities of world exploration centuries ago was that sailors would often die due to a lack of fresh water while caught in the windless waters of the South Atlantic. Eventually, the Spanish Armadas and South American sailors learned where the currents of the mighty Amazon were. Consequently, they were able to instruct ships that had run out of water to drop their buckets in the middle of the South Atlantic into the fresh water currents of the Amazon.

I believe that the local body of believers is that current of fresh water in which we can drop our buckets for refreshment in the midst of our journey carrying Christ to a salty and, sometimes, unreceptive world. Who doesn't need to be reminded of how special they are to God or affirmed for their faith in God? Who doesn't need their parachute packed?

Let me tell you the rest of the story about little Caleb. He's not so little any more! By the grace of God he's a healthy little boy today. It's really quite remarkable how the Lord has allowed humanity to take some giant steps in caring for and nurturing premature babies. But any doctor will tell you that there's no place more suited for the formation of a child than a woman's body. It's been a long road for Rex and Cathy.

It's also been a long road for God the Father in His relationship with His people. Far too many of His children are trying to live as Lone Ranger Christians. George Barna, the influential researcher of religious life in America, reports that in recent years a majority of people who made a first-time "decision" for Christ were no longer connected to a Christian church within just eight weeks of their decision.[3]

I think of the Lone Ranger Christian when I'm in that special wing of the hospital designed for premature babies. This is really what happens to one who practices Lone Ranger Christianity. Their formation is threatened. Indeed, their spiritual lives are at risk.

One of the reasons Jesus came was to destroy the work of the devil (1 John 3:8). Much of what it means to be formed into Christ's image is being fashioned into a warrior who assaults the forces of darkness in this world. God is forming an army of mature soldiers making an impact for the kingdom of God upon our culture. But a large wing of this force has abandoned the disciplines of formation. They have abandoned the body of believers and thus stunted the process of formation into the image of Christ.

According to numerous broad surveys, three-fourths of Americans claim to have made a personal commitment to Jesus Christ as Lord and Savior. So why don't Christians in America make more of an impact? I used to wonder about that. But not any more. The stark reality is that too many of us are practicing Lone Ranger Christianity, leaving God little to work with in regard to forming an army of warriors. What is true biologically is also true spiritually: formation takes place within a body.

Chapter 4

Handle with Care

I'll never forget that feeling the day we packed our things to leave the hospital. West Florida Regional Hospital had been wonderful to us. The labor and delivery nurses were attentive, compassionate, and full of genuine joy for us. The doctor was great. The nurses that looked after Tara and her disheveled husband were thorough and sensitive to every one of our needs. The nurses that worked in the nursery were fabulous. I couldn't help but think that this baby stuff was easier than I had expected. But then it was time for us to leave.

As I pulled the Toyota around to the front of the hospital, loaded it and helped Tara and Skyler get into the car, a horrifying thought gripped me. "None of these people at the hospital are coming home with us!" I suddenly wanted to cry out, "Are you sure you don't want to come home with us?" I don't remember driving slower or more carefully in my life than when I pulled out onto Davis Highway. I can't ever remember being more critical and judgmental of those lunatics buzzing by me as though they were trying to break the sound barrier. This was especially hypocritical when you consider that I'm usually one of those lunatics.

A strange mixture of fear and joy comes with driving off from the hospital with your firstborn in the vehicle. There's a powerful sense of transition and new beginning, and yet fear as well. It's a fear closely attached to the question, "What do I do with this thing?" It's a healthy fear born out of an awareness of the fragility of new life.

It wasn't long before another thought crossed my mind: "This is exactly how God's people should view and care for a new believer." On more than one occasion the New Testament refers to new believers as babies (John 3:5; Heb. 5:12-14). I'm sure you know that babies have soft spots on their heads. These soft spots are places where the bones have not yet grown together. I remember being able to see and feel Skyler's pulse through his soft spot on the top of his head. Any new believer or anyone who has recently rededicated themselves to Christ has some soft spots as well. They are spiritually fragile, learning to live as a whole new creation with new habits and a new perspective. Because of this they need our constant support, attention, and affection.

I recently heard about three ministers in Minnesota who got together for coffee one day. They were talking about the problem of bat infestation in their church buildings. One minister said he got so mad that he took a shotgun to the building. He reported that it had done little good only making holes in the ceiling. The second minister said that he trapped the bats alive, drove them fifty miles outside of town, and released them. Two weeks later they were back in church. The third minister commented that he simply didn't have any more problems with bats. When the others asked what he did, he replied, "I simply baptized them and I haven't seen them since."

It's somewhat sad that we all get the joke. But I think this joke reflects more upon the church than it does the new believer. I've seen church after church pour all their energy into getting people to make "a decision" in regard to placing membership, getting baptized or recommitting themselves to God. At the moment of decision the church expresses tremendous joy and excitement. But within weeks there's a noticeable absence of support, attention and affection for the ones who've made the decision. Ministers and church members are off to recruit others to make "a decision" for Christ.

How many times have churches done the equivalent of leaving a baby on the doorstep hoping someone else will take care of that new baby Christian? More often than not, churches have been guilty of aborting and abandoning new believers through their neglect.

When I consider a local church's responsibility to new believers, I often think of Isaiah 40:11 and how Isaiah describes God. "He tends his flock like a shepherd; He gathers the lambs in his arms and carries them close to his heart." God carries the lambs, the young ones, the ones who can't stand yet, and He carries them close to His heart. They're fragile so He handles them with care.

It's difficult to think of the apostle Paul as a lamb, a young 'un, who had difficulty standing on his own. He wrote almost half of the books that make up the New Testament, and in some of them his personality seems more like a lion than a lamb. But there was a time when Paul was, indeed, a young 'un when it came to the Christian faith. His conversion story in Acts 9:1-19 may be one of the most radical turnabouts recorded in Scripture.

The story that followed his conversion is just as significant (Acts 9:19-31). It happened when Paul was so young in the faith that he still went by his old name, Saul. It didn't take long for Saul's conversion to make front page news in Damascus. This is due to the fact that Saul didn't exactly keep it a secret. Following his conversion he spent several days with the disciples in Damascus, and "at once" (Acts 9:20) began preaching in the synagogues that Jesus was the Son of God.

According to Acts 9:21, the Jews in the synagogues were no less than astonished at what Saul was saying. "Isn't he the same man who raised havoc in Jerusalem among those who call on this name? And hasn't he come here to take them as prisoners to the chief priests?" Here was a man who, only days earlier, had left Jerusalem to travel to Damascus with the intention of dragging any Jews who had confessed their faith in Jesus back to Jerusalem and throwing them in prison (Acts 9:1-2). But now he's preaching the very message that he's been throwing other Jews in jail for believing.

These synagogues in Damascus were probably the very ones in which Saul had received his letters of credit as an official agent of the Jewish faith and of the Sanhedrin. Now, in these very places, Saul is lifting his voice on behalf of the One whom he had been vehemently opposing. It would have been much easier and safer for Saul to have preached first to a people who did not know him or have a record of his past. Instead, Saul stood before those who knew him best and preached a message that just about got him killed. Were it not for some of the believers in Damascus, perhaps he would have been killed. Under the cover of night they sneaked Saul out of town. Unfortunately, though, he had merely sneaked out of the frying pan and into the fire.

After leaving Damascus, he travels only deeper into newfound enemy territory—Jerusalem, the very epicenter of Judaism and opposition against the message of Jesus Christ. Conscious of the word spreading and the threats made on his life, Saul looked to join the group of fellow believers in Jerusalem. When he arrived he tried to join the local church there, "but they were afraid of him, not believing that he really was a disciple" (Acts 9:26).

Instead of open arms, Saul encountered slammed doors. Suddenly he was positioned between bookends of rejection. His former associates, friends and peers rejected him because of his defection. His fellow believers rejected him because they refused to believe that his conversion was authentic and could not forget his former campaign of persecution against them.

Have you ever felt stuck between bookends of rejection? Left out in the cold? Hung out to dry and twisting in the wind? Your soft spots left exposed? Well, I hope that you had what Saul had.

He was Barnabas and his name meant "son of encouragement." Barnabas did indeed live up to his name. He was the hinge upon which the door that was once slammed in Saul's face swung open. Luke writes: "But Barnabas took him and brought him to the apostles. He told them how Saul on his journey had seen the Lord and that the Lord had spoken to him, and how in Damascus he had preached fearlessly in the name of Jesus. So Saul stayed with them and moved about freely in Jerusalem, speaking boldly in the name of the Lord. He talked and debated with the Grecian Jews, but they tried to kill him. When the brothers learned of this, they took him down to Caesarea and sent him off to Tarsus" (Acts 9:27-30). Very early in his Christian experience, Saul learned the place and importance of other believers in his life.

While a relationship with Christ will make you alive (Eph. 2:5), it's a relationship with His followers that will keep you alive, literally and spiritually. In both Damascus and Jerusalem believers came to the aid of Saul and saved his life. We don't know their names, but God does. The one name we do know is Barnabas. Why? I think it's because he came to Saul's aid at a time when he was in a soft spot. It was early in his Christian experience, and he was incredibly vulnerable. If Barnabas hadn't spoken on Saul's behalf to the church in Jerusalem, I wonder if Saul would have been around long enough to have his name changed and write what amounts to almost half of our New Testament. It was Barnabas who made the difference in the believers changing their minds and accepting Saul, eventually helping to save his life when the local religious establishment attempted to kill him.

The next time someone mentions Paul being a giant of the faith, remember Barnabas and how he handled Saul with care when he was in a soft spot. Behind every giant, there's a giant-maker.

Many years ago a girl known as Little Annie lived in a mental institution outside of Boston. Her room was like a dungeon. It received little light and even less hope. According to doctors, it was the only place for those who were hopelessly insane. During Little Annie's time in the dungeon, an elderly nurse who was nearing retirement believed there was hope—even for the "hopeless." She would take her lunch down to the dungeon and eat outside the cell where Little Annie was kept. She felt that she could, perhaps, communicate some love and hope to the little girl.

In many ways Little Annie behaved like an animal. On occasion she would charge at the person sitting outside her cell; other times, she would sit in the corner ignoring her visitor. One day the elderly nurse brought some brownies and left them for her. Little Annie gave no hint that she knew or even cared that they were there, but when the nurse returned the next day, the brownies were gone. Every Thursday, from that time forward, the elderly nurse would bring Little Annie brownies.

Before long doctors in the institution noticed that Little Annie was changing. After a period of time observing her, they decided to "promote" her to another wing of the institution. Eventually this "hopeless" case was told that she could return to her home in the "outside" world. Little Annie refused to go. She wanted to stay and help others who were facing the kind of adversity she once faced. Many years later, it was Little Annie who cared for, taught and nurtured Helen Keller.[4]

Little Annie was Anne Sullivan, and Helen Keller, as I'm sure you know, changed how the world viewed the disabled and challenged. When Helen Keller was in a soft spot, it was Anne Sullivan who handled her with care. When Anne Sullivan was in a soft spot, it was an elderly nurse who handled her with care. The world is a different place today for the physically and mentally challenged because of an anonymous elderly nurse who handled with care someone in a soft spot.

You can be sure God knows that nurse's name and anyone else's name who lives up to the name of Barnabas, a son of encouragement. Keep your eyes open for those with "soft spots." In doing so, you could be helping rescue tomorrow's giants.

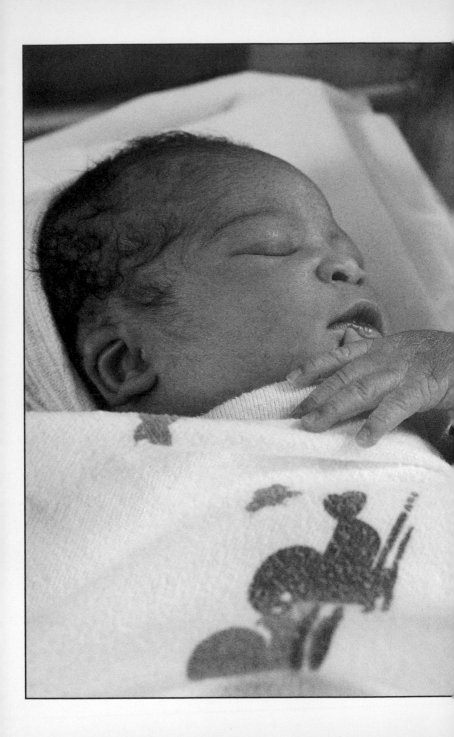

Chapter 5

Get A Grip

Newborns have it good, especially in the first several weeks of their lives. All they do is lie around, eat and sleep. Somebody bathes them, somebody dresses them, somebody changes their diapers, and somebody is always wanting to hold them. Skyler was rarely awake, snoozing through pretty much everything except the growling of his empty stomach. The moments we saw him with his eyes open for any length of time were rare and precious. This is probably why I'll never forget one Saturday afternoon when he was about a month old.

He was unusually alert as I cradled him between my legs. Tara was gone for the afternoon, and for the first time that I could remember I had some significant time alone with my son. I'll never forget looking into his eyes. My heart swelled as I gazed into them. My only wish was that he could understand the depth of my love and passion for him. In fact, the longer I dwelt upon how much I loved him, a strange feeling came over me. It was a feeling of frustration, believe it or not. Frustration born out of an awareness that there was no way for me to convey the depth of my love for him in a way that he could understand.

In that special moment I stumbled upon a glimpse of God's passion for me. "Chris, what Skyler is to you in your arms is what you are to God in His arms. You have no idea how deeply He loves you. Your capacity to understand the depth of His love for you is so minimal and immature. And just as you want Skyler to understand how much you love him, so God wants you to understand how much He loves you. His heart for you beats with frustrated passion, a passion longing for you to see and understand His love for you in all of its fullness."

This glimpse into the Father's heart for me is nothing new or original. Remember what Paul prayed for the believers in Ephesus? "And I pray that you. . . may have power together with all the saints, to grasp how wide and long and high and deep is the love of Christ, and to know this love" (Eph. 3:18).

Just because we're Christians doesn't necessarily mean that we have a full understanding of God's love and affection for us. Paul prayed this prayer on behalf of Christians just like you and me. He's praying that God will give them the capacity to grasp the magnitude of His love for them. Many of us are like children wading around the edge of an ocean. There are depths to this ocean of God's love that we know nothing of, and He longs for us to move into the deeper waters of His love. He wants us to move out to the depths where our feet can't touch the bottom.

When Paul prayed that the Ephesians may be able to grasp God's love, the Greek word he used for "grasp" was the same word used to describe two opponents engaged in a wrestling match. It means literally "to lay hold of." Paul was not so much praying for believers to comprehend God's love in their minds as he was praying for believers to experience God's love in their hearts. Paul wrote that "Christ's love compels me" (2 Cor. 5:14). The Greek word for "compel" means "to be in the grip of something." In other words, Paul was saying, "I'm in the grip of Christ's love." This is a portrait of a man who is himself coming to a greater awareness of God's love and affection for him. The more you seek to lay hold of God's love for you, the more God's love lays hold on you. The more you seek to get a grip on God's love for you, the more God's love gets a grip on you.

The fact that Paul prayed this prayer on behalf of Christians tells me that we need this prayer prayed on our behalf today. The common ground that unites all of us, no matter how different we are from one another, is that we carry within us a deep desire to feel a sense of significance, worth and meaning. We may drink from many different wells to quench that thirst but we all have the same thirst.

This thirst may be the very force upon which our lives run. Men especially have a tendency to seek our sense of significance, worth and meaning through accomplishment. We measure ourselves by salaries, promotions, won/loss columns and all kinds of score-boards and trophies. Why? Because such things bring us other people's attention, affirmation, admiration, esteem and recognition.

A woman's sense of significance, worth and meaning is often derived from her appearance, how well-behaved the kids are, social standing and propriety and a hundred other things. Why? Because such things bring her people's attention, affirmation, admiration, esteem and recognition. While the desire for these things is often noted in the teenage years, the fact is that we never grow out of it.

This thirst becomes a hazard to our spiritual health when we run to anyone or anything else other than our Father in heaven for that sense of significance and worth. This is because our sense of significance, meaning and worth is only as secure as that to which it is tied. Suppose that we derive such things from our occupation. What would happen to our sense of significance, meaning and worth when we lose our occupation due to poor performance, an unjust employer or client, or a disabling accident? What if we derive our worth from our physical appearance and how people respond to us? What would happen if it suddenly changed due to an illness or an accident?

What will happen when it *does* change and time takes its toll on our bodies? What if our sense of self-worth is largely dictated by how a certain someone of the opposite sex responds to us? What would happen if that person no longer feels about us the way we feel about him or her? Our sense of significance, meaning and worth are only as secure as those things to which they are tied, and nothing in this world is secure. Everything changes.

There is one thing that does last forever: "The steadfast love of the Lord never ceases" (Lam. 3:22-23). If our sense of significance, meaning and worth is tied to His love and affection for us then we'll never lose that significance because His love never ceases. Paul celebrates this in Romans 8:35-39: "Who shall separate us from the love of Christ? Shall trouble or hardship or persecution or famine or nakedness or danger or sword?. . . No, in all these things we are more than conquerors through him who loved us. For I am convinced that neither death nor life, neither angels nor demons, neither the present nor the future, nor any powers, neither height nor depth, nor anything else in all creation, will be able to separate us from the love of God that is in Christ Jesus our Lord."

We can't be separated from His love! This is good news if our sense of significance and self-worth is derived from what God thinks about us and how He feels about us. But it's sobering news if our sense of significance and self-worth is tied to anything else. We cannot be separated from the love of God, but we can and eventually will be separated from anything else that gives us our sense of significance and self-worth. Everything changes. The earthquakes will come, the faultlines will shift. And when they do, whatever we have built along the fault will be shaken.

Charles Cooley is considered by many to be the dean of American sociology. He developed the concept of the "looking-glass self." By this he meant that a person's view of himself is established by what he thinks the most important person in his life thinks of him.[5] The most important person on earth to me is my wife. If Tara thinks I'm one handsome hunk, then no matter what anyone else says or how many people say it, I know that I'm one handsome hunk.

This is also true when it comes to our relationship with God. When we're walking in an intimate relationship with Him, and He is the most important person in our lives, what He thinks about us governs our understanding of ourselves. Because the Creator of the universe knows our fingerprints, the number of hairs on our heads, and gave His one and only innocent Son to die on a cross on our behalf, we can know that we are of great significance and worth.

Once we derive our sense of significance and self-worth from the love of God, we are truly free. No longer are we enslaved by the all-consuming desire to achieve more, be wanted more or have more in an attempt to solidify our sense of significance and self-worth. From this point on we can live out of our sense of significance and self-worth and no longer in an effort to obtain a sense of significance and self-worth. No longer will we have to compromise ourselves morally and ethically in order to get or keep those things or persons from which we derive our sense of significance and self-worth. Rather we are truly free to submit to what God wants no matter the cost or what may change in our lives. Our sense of significance and self-worth is no longer at stake. It is already established in God's love and affection.

No one loves us as much as God loves us. No one believes in us as deeply as God believes in us. No one has died for us like God's Son has died for us. No one can love us as perfectly and completely as God loves us because He is love (I John 4:7). This is why no one and nothing but His love will ultimately satisfy and stabilize us.

Do you see why it's so important to ask God to enable us to get a grip on His love for us? When's the last time you prayed to get a grip? As a golfer I've always been amused by some of the phrases golfers use. A popular one these days that I see on bumper stickers is "Grip It And Rip It" which calls for the golfer to "throw caution to the wind" and just swing hard (suicide for a golf swing, but I'll leave that for the professionals to explain). But it's a good phrase when it comes to the love of God. If we can get a grip on it, we can "rip" in it: "Rest In Peace." We can rest in the peace of God's love for us and live out of that quiet, solid center.

Chapter 6

Safety Gates

When Skyler got to moving on "all fours" with about the speed and maneuverability of a four wheeler, we would, on occasion, set up a safety gate in our living room. This portable plastic divider gave Skyler his own space in the living room to play, but it also limited his freedom to roam throughout the rest of the house while we were busy doing other things. It's amazing what a child his age will do with unrestricted freedom and opportunity.

I can't tell you the number or variety of things that I've found in his mouth from time to time. Skyler has experimented with everything from quarters, to the sports page, to athletic socks. Do you ever remember hearing that in the event of a nuclear holocaust the only edible things we could rely upon for nourishment were a few household insects? Well, on more than one occasion, we found Skyler preparing for a nuclear holocaust. Maybe he knows something that the rest of us don't and is just conditioning himself for the inevitable consumption of such critters. And I can't begin to tell you what I've found in his hands, but you probably can imagine if you've had small children. What toddler doesn't like to dig in plants and play with electrical cords?

These are some of the reasons why, every now and then, we would put up the safety gate. We wanted to give him his own space but also restrict him from having too much freedom and opportunity. With too much freedom Skyler could explore things that he really didn't know how to handle and, because of that, hurt himself. He didn't understand why we erected the safety gate. It probably seemed like more of a fence to him. All he could see was that there were times when daddy wouldn't let him be where he wanted to be or do what he wanted to do. He couldn't see how our love for him led us to limit him.

I suspect that the same could be said about us when it comes to our relationship with our Father in heaven. If I had a nickel for every time I've heard someone quote I Corinthians 10:13, I'd be one wealthy fella. You may not recognize the reference, but you will recognize the scripture: "And God is faithful; he will not let you be tempted beyond what you can bear." We usually cite this passage when we want to convey the thought that God limits the weight of adversity He allows people to experience. This is indeed true and temptation does often manifest itself in the context of adversity in our lives.

But I don't believe this verse just refers to the level of adversity God allows us to experience. It could also be that God places limitations on the amount of prosperity, opportunity and freedom which He allows us to experience. After all, temptation can be present in prosperity, opportunity and freedom just as it is in adversity—if not more so. There are probably some things in life we really want right now but that God, in His wisdom, sees that we really can't handle. If we did have them their weight would be more than we could bear. We would end up being hurt physically, mentally, emotionally or spiritually.

Solomon understood how an abundance of prosperity, opportunity and freedom can pose problems. This is why he wrote: "Give me neither poverty nor riches, but give me only my daily bread. Otherwise I may have too much and disown you and say, 'Who is the Lord?' Or I may become poor and steal, and so dishonor the name of my God" (Prov. 30:8-9). God knows our limitations in facing prosperity as well as adversity, and His love for us is at the heart of his limitations of us. The last thing He wants is to allow us opportunity that we can't handle and for us to end up with something lodged in our spiritual windpipes that slowly chokes the spiritual life out of us.

So every now and then God puts up a safety gate in our lives to keep us from going where we want to go but really can't handle going. It may seem like a fence. But it's really a safety gate. The next time you're standing there gripping one of those safety gates and wailing at the top of your lungs, try to understand what my little boy can't right now. The Father is limiting you because he loves you. Besides, weren't you the one who prayed "and lead me not into temptation"? Life's safety gates are often God's answers to such prayers.

Chapter 7

The Glob

It was on the first Sunday morning of December that I ventured over Skyler's safety gate and into his territory. It was well past time for me to leave and get to the church building, but I couldn't resist. I was headed out the door but had to go through the living room to pick up my car keys, and when I did, he caught my eye. My baby boy was in the corner of the living room completely absorbed in his play. He was lost in the fascination of blocks, board books, plastic key chains, teething rings and golf balls.

Though I was already in my Sunday "dress duds"—a new suit, I might add—I quietly made my way over to the safety gate, hiked one leg over and then the other, eventually getting on "all fours" to sneak up on him. I'll finish the story in just a moment, but first let me digress.

Christmas was already on my mind as I was crawling over to him, so it didn't surprise me when the analogy struck me. Wasn't what I was doing exactly what God did in and through Jesus? Though He was dressed in garments of righteousness, holiness and splendor, He scaled the fence separating humanity from divinity, got down on the ground, and crawled over into our little corner of the universe on His hands and knees where we could look Him in the eyes. And He did it for the same reason I was doing it that December morning—to be in joyful fellowship with His children.

The coming of Jesus Christ is the greatest example of God's desire to be in an intimate relationship with human beings. But it's not the only one. In fact, it's one of many efforts God has made to live with and among us. The Bible in essence is a resume of God's grand and continual efforts to be with His people. Genesis 3 records Him actually walking in the garden of Eden in the cool of the evening looking for Adam and Eve. Exodus 26 records God instructing Moses to build a portable tabernacle so that as His people journeyed through the wilderness to the Promised Land His manifest presence could dwell in their midst. The early chapters of 1 Kings tell the story of Solomon building a magnificent temple in Jerusalem where God's manifest presence could dwell among His people. The gospels tell us of God's presence coming to dwell among us in the form of a temple of flesh and bones, Jesus Christ, Immanuel, "God with us" (Matt. 1:23). And beginning at Pentecost God now dwells not just among us but within us through His precious Holy Spirit, thereby making us His temples (1 Cor. 6:19).

From beginning to end the Scriptures testify that God longs to dwell in an intimate relationship with us. This story of intimacy begins in a garden in Genesis and will eventually culminate in an eternal garden according to Revelation 22. In between these two points lies the story of God's passionate efforts to live in intimacy with His people. He longs to be with us so desperately, in fact, that not only did He seek to live with us through the life of Jesus but also through the death of Jesus. "He died for us so that, whether we are awake or asleep, we may live together with him" (I Thess. 5:10). God longs to live with us—in our lives before the grave (awake) and beyond the grave (asleep).

But I wonder if I react to God's overtures the same way Skyler reacted to me that Sunday morning. I crawled over to him, so close that he could feel my breath on his neck. He whirled around, saw me and leaped in my direction, throwing his arms up and around my neck as best he could, burying his head in the lapel of my coat. I soaked in the moment.

Indeed, I was soaked in more ways than one. As he pulled his head away from my coat and looked up at me with a grin that could steal the Grinch's heart, I couldn't help but notice the deposit that he had left on my new suit. It was…well…what you would expect to come out of the runny nose of your little one. It was …er…a glob—alright, a glob of gunk. And it was mobile, heading south down the lapel of my coat. My spotless suit wasn't so spotless anymore. It was still worth it, though, and I would do it all over again this coming Sunday morning. My son turning around and receiving me makes all the difference in the world.

The way Skyler reacted to my pursuit and presence is exactly how God longs for us to react to His pursuit and presence. In the midst of our preoccupation with our toys, work, dreams and regrets, He crawls over the fence, gets down on "all fours" and pursues us until we feel His breath on the back of our necks. The question is whether or not we will turn around and receive Him. This is literally what the word "repent" means—to do an "about face," to turn around and bury yourself in Him. Bury yourself—that's a good term. We bury that which is dead. When we repent and turn to Him we are making a commitment to die to ourselves and live for Him.

The apostle Paul says that this burial of ourselves is expressed in baptism when we are buried in Christ and with Christ (Rom. 6:1-4). And what happened to me when Skyler buried his face in my coat is exactly what happens to Christ when we bury ourselves in Him—a glob of gunk is transferred from us to Him. The gunk of our sin is transferred to Him. He's stained with it. When God then looks at His Son, He sees His Son as having committed the sins that we committed, and therefore His Son suffers the curse that comes with being stained— separation from God through death upon the cross.

But something else is also transferred from Jesus to us—His perfection and righteousness. "You are all sons of God through faith in Christ Jesus, for all of you who were baptized into Christ have clothed yourselves with Christ" (Gal. 3:26-27). When we bury ourselves in Him, we are clothed in His perfection and righteousness, and He gets stained with the gunk of our sin. God looks upon us and sees us as Jesus actually is—perfect, obedient, holy, righteous, and unblemished. God looks upon Jesus and sees Him as we actually are - imperfect, disobedient, unholy, unrighteous and blemished. So Jesus gets the cross, and we get to live together with God as His sons and daughters.

This is why God crawled over the fence and why He continues to crawl over the fences that we erect in order to keep our distance from Him and maintain our own space. He longs to live in intimacy with each one of us, so desperately that He's willing to take on the gunk of our sin and give us the cloak of His righteousness. All we need to do is turn around. He's right there on "all fours" at eye level with a smile of anxious anticipation.

Chapter 8

Cheerios or Cold Green Beans?

One Saturday morning I was sitting at the kitchen table having breakfast with Skyler. We were eating the same thing, Cheerios, though they were prepared differently according to our likings. I was eating out of a bowl while Skyler was eating off the table. I was having my Cheerios "wet" while Skyler was having his "dry"—"very dry" in fact. I was managing to get the majority of mine in my mouth while Skyler was managing to get the majority of his everywhere but in his mouth.

There are times after Skyler gets done eating when it appears as though our kitchen has become some kind of culinary war zone, a veritable "no man's land." Of course, I've been told by many women that it's difficult to find a man in the kitchen after a meal, but that's not what I mean when I use the term "no man's land" in regard to Skyler.

This Saturday, however, I wasn't concerned with the kitchen being transformed into "no man's land." The Pensacola *News Journal* sports page had my attention. I was catching up on the world of sports when I felt a small hand patting my arm. I looked over and there was Skyler, holding a Cheerio up to my mouth.

This was a significant moment believe it or not. It wasn't the first time that Skyler had attempted to feed me. He had tried to feed me before with things far less tasty than a Cheerio. He was generous with everyone when it came to sharing his broccoli, carrots and cold green beans, but he never got around to offering anybody his Cheerios.

I tilted my head, opened my mouth, and Skyler inserted his entire hand in order to deposit the Cheerio. With as big a mouth as some people say I have, it wasn't that much of a stretch for me. He had a huge smile on his face when he left his deposit, and I couldn't help but smile as well.

I never finished reading the sports page that morning but ate the rest of my breakfast out of his hand. I certainly could feed myself a lot more efficiently than he could. But there was something special about my boy making an effort to feed me by hand something that was precious to him after months of me feeding him by hand.

Our Father in heaven must feel the same way when we offer Him something of our own free will after all the years and ways in which He's blessed us. How precious it must be when He feels a hand patting Him on the arm and sees us with an offering in our hands and smiles on our faces. It isn't that God can't live without the praise, thanksgiving, love, affection, adoration and offering of our lives. It's just that He doesn't want to live without such things any more than I want to live without such things from my son.

In the Old Testament one of the ways the people of God expressed their devotion and thanksgiving to God was through an animal sacrifice known as a "freewill offering." It was a voluntary sacrifice motivated out of thanksgiving for what God had done in their lives. A "freewill offering" is, in essence, what I received from Skyler, and that was why I was so touched. It was something he did of his own initiative and choice. This is what God longs to receive from His people, and when He does, it touches Him deeply.

I wonder if Paul had the concept of a "freewill offering" in mind when he wrote Romans 12:1: "Therefore, I urge you, brothers, in view of God's mercy, to offer your bodies as living sacrifices, holy and pleasing to God—this is your spiritual act of worship." In view of God's mercy, as a response to God's mercy, we offer ourselves as living sacrifices, and this becomes our spiritual act of worship. Our very lives are "freewill offerings" to God, made to Him in view of His mercy in our lives.

Psalm 116:15 says, "Precious in the sight of the Lord is the death of his saints." This verse is most likely referring to physical death. But I can't help but consider that it's a precious thing in God's sight when His people die to themselves, to their own selfish desires and live for Him, what He wants them to do, and how He wants them to live. Ephesians 5:2 says that Christ "gave Himself up... as a fragrant offering and sacrifice to God."

We tend to think of worship as what transpires in an assembly with other believers on Sunday mornings. Romans 12:1 has nothing to do with what goes on among an assembly of believers on Sunday mornings, but has everything to do with the lives of believers Monday through Saturday. "Offer your bodies as living sacrifices, holy and pleasing to God—this is your spiritual act of worship." It's entirely probable that the "freewill offering" God most desires from us is not necessarily the offering of our lips for one hour on Sunday mornings, but the offering of our moral and ethical lives Monday through Saturday.

Years ago around Thanksgiving, Paul Harvey told millions of Americans the sadly comical but all-too-true story of a phone call received by a nationally recognized poultry company. In November of every year they operated a toll-free 800 number for Americans to call who had questions about how to prepare their holiday turkeys. One woman called asking how long was "too long" for a turkey to be frozen and yet still edible. For almost two decades she had kept one in her freezer—the same one. The customer service representative said that it still might be fine to eat but didn't want to say for sure. The woman replied, "Well, I'll just give this one to the church and go get a fresh one."

This wasn't the first time, nor will it be the last time, that God gets the leftovers. It's a sad but common reality that when His people have made "freewill offerings" they often have done it with the leftovers of their lives—the things that aren't really all that precious to them and don't cost them much either. Do you remember what David, a man after God's own heart, once said? "I will not....sacrifice a burnt offering that costs me nothing" (1 Chron. 21:24).

I must confess that there have been too many times when I've offered God something that cost me nothing.

There are plenty of times in my life when I've offered God nothing of what was precious to me and everything that meant little to me. It's easy to sing songs on Sunday mornings because it doesn't cost me much. It's far more difficult and costly to live up to the promises I made in those songs.

The day Skyler offered me his Cheerios was significant because he offered me something precious to him. For once, he wasn't offering me his broccoli, his carrots or his cold green beans, but he was offering me something as precious as life itself to a toddler—his Cheerios. It doesn't impress me when he offers me a cold green bean. But when he offers me a Cheerio it does, because he's giving me back something that I've given him which has become precious to him.

What's precious to you? Your time? Your treasure? Your talents? Have you been giving God your cold green beans? Don't you think He deserves your Cheerios?

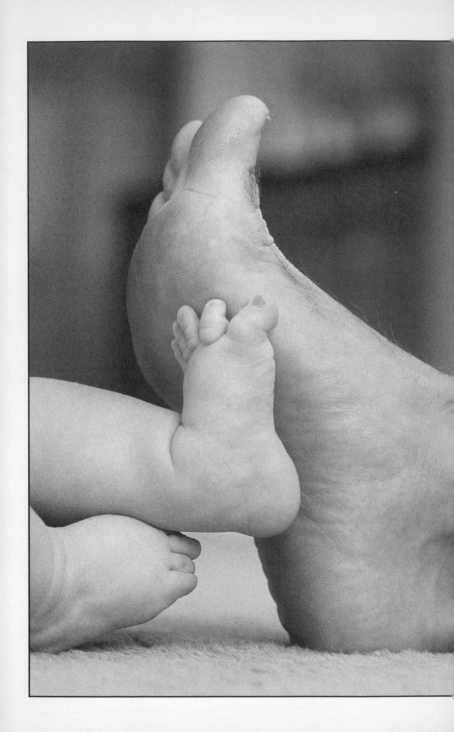

Chapter 9

A Can of Happy

Lately Skyler and I have been playing with his blocks in the living room. He's at that age where he's learning about shapes, sizes and colors. One of the activities he loves is to drop differently shaped blocks through their correspondingly shaped holes in the lid of a plastic yellow cylinder.

He's still learning, though, to match the shape of the blocks with the shape of the holes and every once in a while grows quite frustrated when he can't jam a block through a hole that's not cut out for that particular block. The frustration escalates quickly. He goes from sitting down to standing up and trying to force the square through the triangle. And when it doesn't work, the cheeks redden, the tears flow, he hollers and the cylinder goes flyin' across the room.

Watching my son's frustration in trying to jam a square block through a triangular hole is an appropriate picture of what we try to do as adults from time to time. I think we all go through seasons in our lives when we try to cram things into the cylinder of our souls that our souls just weren't cut out for. Frustration and exasperation ensue. And the longer we try forcing, jamming and cramming such things into our souls, the more frustration and exasperation spills out of our spirits and into our lives. Our souls were cut out for one specific thing, and only that specific thing can smoothly fit and properly fill the cylinder of our souls.

A few Christmases ago I asked a good friend of mine, a few years older than me, what he wanted for Christmas. He responded half-jokingly, "A can of happy, I suppose." For several moments an awkward silence filled the truck in which we rode. The moment he said that, it was as though both of us realized that there was a seed of truth in his off-handed comment. Jesus Himself said that it was out of the overflow of our hearts that we speak (Lk. 6:45). Our mouths so often serve as flare guns, firing flares into the night looking for help as we come to grips with a loss of direction and orientation in the midst of life's troubled waters.

By the world's standards my friend had everything one could ever want. He had achieved many of his dreams and goals. His standard of living was one that most Americans only dream of. But he was coming to the realization that achieving a standard of living could not be equated with experiencing a quality of life. His lack of fulfillment and satisfaction finally bubbled up and spilled out of his mouth in the form of a joking confession that if happiness could be canned, he'd buy a six pack of it.

Material provision, in all of its many forms, doesn't meet the needs of the soul—which is why it's possible to have too much to live on and yet not enough to live for. There is a difference between making a living and having a life. A person can have everything he wants and yet almost nothing he really needs. It's sadly ironic that though America is the most prosperous nation in the history of the world, it is filled nevertheless with an abundance of spiritually impoverished people—among whom I would place myself from time to time.

It was in my junior year that I tore the cartilage in my right knee while playing defensive back on the high school football team. I would like to say that I had hurt it making a valiant, heroic play in the waning seconds of a championship game, but the truth is I hurt it in the pre-game warm-ups. For the next six weeks, my right leg was in a cast, and I hobbled around on crutches. I'll never forget what my leg looked like when the doctor finally removed the cast. It seemed as if my arm was twice the width of my leg; in fact, the more I looked at my leg, the more it resembled a stilt.

My orthopedic doctor could see that I was horrified by the sight, and he mercifully explained to me that my leg had undergone muscle atrophy. Muscle atrophy occurs when your muscles decay from lack of use. My leg was designed for the purpose of supporting and transporting me. When I was not able to use it for several weeks, in accordance with its designed and intended purpose, its muscles decayed from lack of use.

What happened to my leg is what happens to our spirits or souls when we do not allow ourselves to function according to our designed purpose. We decay, we suffer atrophy of the soul. We were created for the purpose of living in an intimate relationship with God. Paul said it is in God that we "live and move and have our being" (Acts 17:28). And Jesus said, "Blessed [happy] are those who hunger and thirst for righteousness," and then in the very next phrase spoke of why this was true—"for they will be filled." God created us for the express purpose of living in an intimate relationship with Him. To hunger and thirst for anything else but

God is to settle for a lifetime of emptiness and the continual growls of a hungry soul.

Augustine prayed, "Our hearts are restless until they find their rest in you."[6] Our souls were cut out and custom-made for God, and God alone, to fill. Fulfillment and contentment in life have little do with what we have around us and much more to do with who we have within us.

The prison experiences of the Apostle Paul highlight this basic truth. Consider what he writes from prison: "I am not saying this because I am in need, for I have learned to be content whatever the circumstances. I know what it is to be in need, and I know what it is to have plenty. I have learned the secret of being content in any and every situation, whether well fed or hungry, whether living in plenty or in want. I can do everything through him who gives me strength" (Phil. 4:11-13).

How many times have we all seen that last verse quoted in a weight room at school or in the midst of raising money to build a church building? While I have no qualms with quoting such a verse in those places or times, the truth is that Paul's comments have far more to do with our capacity to experience contentment and satisfaction in life than they do with our capacity to bench press or build church buildings. Paul is able to be content, fulfilled and satisfied in any and every situation, whether living in plenty or in want, because of His relationship with Jesus Christ. The "secret" is not prosperity or poverty. I've seen more than my share of people living in plenty and in want who were unfulfilled and experiencing atrophy of the soul. The "secret" is an intimate relationship with God through Christ Jesus. Fulfillment and contentment in life have little to do with what we have around us and more to do with who we have within us.

But if God created us to live in an intimate relationship with Him then why doesn't He just make us live in an intimate relationship with Him? Why does He create us "batteries not included"? Because God is just like any of us when it comes to love. I loved Tara so much that I wasn't going to force her to marry me. I wanted to be chosen and wanted by her. I had no interest in spending my life with someone upon whom I had forced my will, someone precluded from exercising her free will. That would be robotics, not love.

In the same way God will seek us out, flirt with us, pursue us, court us, try to get our attention and affection until the day we die. But He will not force Himself upon any of us. Love is expressed most plainly in the exercise of free will. We are free to choose, and God created us to do so. But while we are free to choose, we are not free to choose the consequences of our choice. Whether or not we choose to live in an intimate relationship with God has everything to do with whether or not we will function according to our designed purpose and, consequently, "be filled"—or suffer an atrophy of the soul.

Unfortunately we try to fill our souls with a myriad of other things ranging from careers, to titles, to promotions, to money, to popularity, to fame, to busyness, to religion, to relationships, to hobbies, to raw all-out pleasure-seeking experiences. The more we make, achieve, accumulate, experience and possess without God, the more aware we become of the emptiness and the more exasperated we become with our peculiar inability to fill the emptiness.

I once read about a movie in which some ship-wrecked men were left drifting aimlessly on the ocean in a lifeboat. Their rations of food and fresh water were depleted and they were growing deliriously thirsty. One night, while the others were asleep, one man ignored all the serious warnings and instructions of the others and gulped down some ocean water, only to die soon after. Ocean water contains seven times more salt than the human body can safely ingest. When a person drinks it, he is actually accelerating the dehydration process because the kidneys require extra water to flush the salt from his body. The more ocean water one drinks, the thirstier one gets and the sooner one will die of thirst.[7]

This also explains why we can be so exhausted after traveling by plane. Did you know that at an altitude of 30,000 feet an airplane cabin is thirty times as arid as a desert? This is why we usually are so thirsty on our flights. The flight attendants, then, come around and put what on our trays? Peanuts, pretzels or other salty snacks, which only increase our thirst and require extra water to flush out the salt. So what do they offer us to drink? Sodium-filled sodas and caffeinated coffee which both serve to dry us out all the more. When we consume these things in an effort to suppress our appetites or quench our thirst, we only accelerate the dehydration process all the more. Airplanes are basically airborne beef jerky plants traveling 500 miles per hour. We arrive at our destination dehydrated, worn-out, some of us nauseous and others of us with headaches because we never consumed what we really needed—fresh water.

What can happen to us physiologically can also happen to us spiritually—we can die of thirst. We can try to quench our thirst for contentment and fulfillment with a myriad of things we want, but it will never be quenched until we take in the one thing we really need—the living water of a relationship with God through Jesus Christ. Speaking of water, do you remember what Jesus said to one woman who had tried to quench her thirst for contentment through relationships with one man after another? "Everyone who drinks this water will be thirsty again, but whoever drinks the water I give him will never thirst" (John 4:13-14).

Are you tired of trying to jam a square through the shape of a triangle? Are you wiped out from a life of working to consume everything you want and yet finding nothing you really need? Does a "can of happy" sound pretty good to you about now? Are you dying of thirst? It's time to go back to the one and only well that can quench your thirst. Jesus is the only shape that can fit your soul and the only substance that can fill your soul.

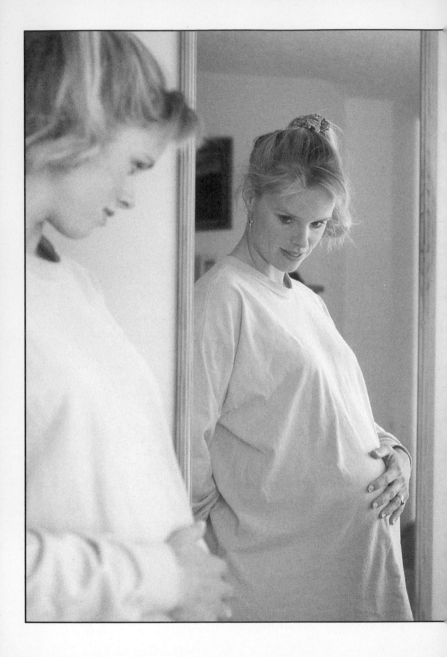

Chapter 10

Conception and Formation

I heard about a father who wanted to show his four-year-old little boy one of the great wonders of life. He took him out to a pasture on the family's ranch and allowed the boy to witness a cow giving birth to a calf. For more than an hour the boy watched with wide-eyed wonder as his father and a local veterinarian came to the aid of the cow and her newborn. The father couldn't help but be tickled at his son's amazement. In the midst of the experience he asked his little boy if he had any questions. The little boy replied, "Well, just one. How fast do you think that calf was going when he ran into that cow?"

Nothing seems quite as miraculous as the process of conception to birth. It's so wondrous that it's difficult for little minds and even big minds to…well…um…conceive. It amazes me when I consider that my 23 pound baby boy was once no bigger than a single cell inside my wife's body. Now that I think about it, I'm even more amazed that all 185 pounds of me was once no bigger than a single cell inside my mother's body.

When I consider my little boy's growth over the last 18 months of his life outside the womb and the preceding nine months in the womb, the words of a song by the late Rich Mullins come to mind: "We are frail, we are fearfully and wonderfully made, forged in the fires of human passion."[8] Skyler's conception happened in a moment of passion between two people in a marital covenant with one another. But while his conception may have happened in a moment, his formation happened over nine months and is still taking place today.

What is true biologically is also true spiritually. Spiritual conception can happen in a moment, but spiritual formation happens over time. In only a moment one can be conceived in Christ. Jesus referred to this experience as being "born again" (John 3:3). The Apostle Paul used the term "new creation" to refer to one who had entered into a relationship with God through Christ Jesus (2 Cor. 5:17). The moment we receive Jesus as our Lord and Savior we become that "new creation." We are conceived in Christ. But as it took time for Skyler to be formed once he was conceived, so it takes time for us to be formed into the image of Christ once we are conceived in Christ.

This truth speaks volumes to those of us weighted down under an anvil of discouragement over our slow development in Christ. We've experienced conception in Christ and are making efforts to put ourselves into position for God to form us into Christ's image. We're immersing ourselves in Scripture, giving ourselves over to frequent prayer, engaging in relationships with other believers, and seeking to serve and minister to others in His name.

But we frequently grow discouraged that we're not where we want or need to be spiritually. We're just not bearing the abundance of spiritual fruit we thought we'd be bearing by now. We don't exactly have bushels of the Spirit's fruit: love, joy, peace, patience, kindness, goodness, faithfulness, gentleness and self-control (Gal. 5:22). When we evaluate the success or faithfulness of our spiritual lives, we feel like the fella who prayed, "Dear Lord, so far today I've done alright. I haven't gossiped, been greedy, grumpy, nasty, selfish or over-indulgent. I'm really glad about that. But in a few minutes, God, I'm going to get out of bed and from then on I'm probably going to need a lot more help." Aren't there times in our lives when that prayer just about sums it up?

We live in a day of instant coffee, microwave dinners, electronic mail, diet pills, fast food, instant relief, overnight deliveries and express check-out lanes at the grocery stores. Fiber optics and microchips have turned airplanes, hotel rooms and homes into offices. Cellular phones and pagers make it possible for us to be immediately accessible anywhere at any time. Our automobiles are actually capable of becoming our home and our office with cellular phones, portable fax machines, compact disc stereo systems and now even microwaves custom-made for cars.

While all of these modern technological conveniences may serve us well, they also have helped to nurture a generation of people who hate to wait. Do you remember the old saying "It's my way or the highway"? Well, these days "our way is the highway." We live our lives in the fast lanes of urgency and on the freeways of immediacy. We're constantly trying to "do this" faster, "get there" quicker, and "have that" more immediately. Patience has become a rare commodity among us. Urgency, immediacy and demand have become the familiar rhythms of our everyday lives.

This infectious spirit of immediacy has become so much a part of the air we breathe that a few of us sometimes decide that if we can't get what we want, when we want it, then we won't have it at all. Before long the spirit of immediacy spills over into our spiritual lives. It's quite easy to become discouraged if one expects significant spiritual change and transformation in the length of time it takes to heat up some leftovers.

Both Jesus and the Apostle Paul have something to say about spiritual growth to those of us immersed in the powerful currents of immediacy. They both liken the dynamics of spiritual growth to the world of agriculture. In the parable of the growing seed Jesus describes how the reign of God grows, whether in this world or in the life of a particular individual. "A man scattered seed on the ground. Night and day, whether he sleeps or gets up, the seed sprouts and grows, though he does not know how. All by itself the soil produces grain—first the stalk, then the head, then the full kernel in the head" (Mk. 4:26-29). Jesus is painting a portrait of process. The reign or rule of God within a person is something that grows gradually.

What does this say to those of us swept along in the powerful currents of immediacy? It says that when it comes to spiritual growth we must learn to exchange our stopwatches for calendars. Sometimes when it comes to growing spiritually and surrendering more and more of our lives to the reign and rule of God we expect too much of ourselves and others too quickly. Often we expect ourselves to take giant steps in a day. If we fail, we are disappointed, frustrated and perhaps even aggravated. Maybe we even tend to write off our disappointment, frustration or aggravation as a sign of righteous indignation. The truth is that we could just be evaluating spiritual growth with a stopwatch instead of a calendars.

In the midst of the raging current of immediacy Jesus calls our attention to the natural world in order to teach us a lesson about the spiritual world. He says the reign, the rule, the work of God is something that grows gradually in a person—"first the stalk, then the head, then the full kernel in the head." It's a process of gradual growth.

A few years ago I heard a story about a man named Hank who had taken on a job as a landscape contractor. He didn't want to appear to be the amateur that he knew he was, so he attempted to project an image of nonchalance, competence and even expertise. One of his first jobs was blasting out some tree stumps with dynamite for a farmer. The problem was that he really didn't know how much dynamite would be needed to do the job. He certainly wasn't going to ask anyone for advice, so he packed what he thought to be enough dynamite under the first stump. He quietly breathed a prayer, looked at the farmer confidently, and pushed down the plunger. The stump shot out of the ground with a resounding "boom" and arched magnificently in the direction of Hank's pickup truck, eventually landing upon and demolishing the roof of the cab. In a flash the farmer turned to Hank and said, "Son, you didn't miss it by much. With a little more practice you'll be able to land those suckers in your truck bed every time."

One doesn't become a landscape specialist in a day. Nobody learns a new language over night. A professional athlete isn't made in a week. Michael Jordan was cut from his tenth grade basketball team. Dr. Seuss' first book was turned down by 23 publishers. In 1905, the University of Bern rejected Albert Einstein's Ph.D. dissertation saying it was irrelevant and fanciful. Henry Ford went bankrupt twice during his first three years in the automobile business. Chester Carlson searched for years before he found backers for his Xerox photocopying process. Michelangelo endured seven years lying on his back on a scaffold to paint the Sistine Chapel.

One of the most successful writers of the 1970s became interested in writing while serving in the Navy. For eight years he wrote a pile of routine reports. When he returned to civilian work he wrote an abundance of stories and articles that never got published. It wasn't until years later that he wrote a book that touched the world. Alex Haley and *Roots* will not be forgotten.

My golf instructor in high school was an elderly gentleman named Harvey Penick. He taught the game of golf for more than seven decades. His only claim was to have seen more golf shots than anyone else ("and too many of them were my own"). It wasn't until he was well into his eighties that he penned the best-selling sports instruction book of all-time. The Little Red Book was, in essence, a collection of notes he had made about the game of golf for several decades.

You no doubt recognize most of these names. But how about the "giants" of the faith? The Bible is laced with examples of people growing gradually and making their most significant contributions to the kingdom of God late in life. Abraham was 75 years old when God promised that he would be the father of many and that all the nations of the world would be blessed through him and his offspring. Twenty-five years later, when Abraham hit the century mark, Isaac was born. Abraham was 100 and God's promises were just beginning to be fulfilled!

Moses was raised as Egyptian royalty during the first 40 years of his life. He then spent the second 40 years of his life in a desert as a consequence of a very bad decision. He didn't receive his call from God or embark on his call until he was at least 80 years old! But somehow I think that his time receiving the finest education in Egypt and his time learning about how to live in a desert proved to be incredibly instrumental in his leadership of the Israelites out of Egyptian bondage, across a wilderness and to the edge of the Promised Land.

What about the Apostle John? He was an aged man, banished to life on a deserted island, when he made his greatest contribution to the kingdom of God. What he saw in a vision he wrote down for others to read. For the last two thousand years, the book of Revelation has inspired countless believers to radical commitment to the Lordship of Jesus Christ in the face of evil and persecution.

There are no instant harvests in the natural world or the spiritual world. We may live in a culture of microwave dinners, but there's no such thing as microwave maturity. Just as a farmer would never look for or judge a harvest immediately after sowing his seeds, so with the seeds of the Kingdom. When you are discouraged take heart in the words of the Apostle Paul: "And we...are being transformed in his likeness with ever-increasing glory, which comes from the Lord, who is the Spirit" (2 Cor. 3:18). Notice that Paul said "are being" and not "have been." Conception happens in a moment, but formation takes time.

H.O. Davidson was a renowned headmaster of the English boarding school Harrow. Regarding one young man in his school, Davidson wrote: "He is forgetful, careless, unpunctual, irregular in every way. He is unable to conquer his slovenliness. He will never make a success." Fortunately Winston Churchill read other things and heard other voices. H. O. Davidson conducted his evaluation of Churchill with a stopwatch instead of a calendar. Let's not make the same mistake in regard to ourselves or others.

Chapter 11

Mistaken For Jesus

―――――――――――――――

Right now Tara and I are engaged in the tedious task of teaching Skyler to tell us what he wants in some way other than whining. Few things are more annoying than my precious little boy whining with the dogged persistence of a jackhammer as he pleads his case. In fact, the whining is infectious. Before long I find myself whining about his whining.

I suppose most of us go through a stage as children where our motto appears to be "rise and whine." And some of us, unfortunately, have difficulty growing out of it. A toddler who whines may be tolerated for a while, but an adult who whines won't. Helping Skyler learn to communicate in some way other than whining is part of his maturation as a human being.

As it is with Skyler, so it is with all of us. There comes a time when we must grow up, especially in our spiritual lives. In the previous chapter I focused on the difference between conception and formation. Some of us have gone about our Christian lives as though conception is all there is to the Christian experience. Our spiritual progression or walk with God came to a halt when we were baptized or joined a local church or had a milestone experience of "getting right with God."

We have abandoned the process of continually putting ourselves in position to be steadily transformed into the image of Jesus Christ. Our behaviors haven't changed. Our attitudes haven't changed. Our language hasn't changed. We're the same people we were when we got baptized, joined that church or had that milestone experience with God. We've settled for conception, abandoned the process of formation, and are stuck in the morass of spiritual apathy and indifference.

The Apostle Paul agonized over this timeless problem of Christians being conceived and yet not fully formed into the image of Jesus Christ. "My dear children, for whom I am again in the pains of childbirth until Christ is formed in you…you were running a good race. Who cut in on you and kept you from obeying the truth?" (Gal. 4:19 and 5:7).

I suppose the reasons for abandoning the process of formation vary from individual to individual. I do have a hunch about one common reason. I think the problem is rooted in a faulty understanding of the essence of Christianity. Many people believe that getting access into heaven after we die is all that Christianity is about. Churches today are full of people who believe that being a Christian means going to church while they're alive and being saved after they die.

The truth is that there's far more to Christianity than eternal life after we die. Consider these words of Paul: "This grace was given us in Christ Jesus before the beginning of time, but it has now been revealed through the appearing of our Savior, Christ Jesus, who has destroyed death and has brought life and immortality to light through the gospel" (2 Tim. 1:9-10). Did you catch that? Jesus came not just to bring "immortality to light through the gospel," but "life...to light through the gospel."

Jesus did not just come so that we could have eternal life after we die. He also came so that we could learn how to "have a life" before we die. He came so that we could have a pattern for how to live, to teach us what to embrace in life and what to avoid, how to go about our relationships, as single adults or married people. He came to show us how to handle our money, our worries, our fears, our critics and our anger. He came not just to give us access to eternal life after we die, but to show us how to have a quality life before we die. We can taste the fruits of the Spirit—love, joy and peace—in this life because they are a by-product of being transformed into the image of Christ.

I think I'm somewhat to blame for fostering the idea that Christianity has more to offer you after you die than before you die. I've emphasized, along with other churches and ministers, the importance of "getting right with God" before you die so that you can go to heaven after you die. No doubt this is a valid motive for restoring one's relationship with God. After all, when Jesus spoke about such a thing, He often referred to our eternal destiny being at stake.

But this isn't the only thing at stake when making a decision as to whether or not to enter into an intimate relationship with God through Jesus Christ. Life "before the grave" and not just "beyond the grave" is at stake as well. Jesus came to bring "life and immortality to light through the gospel." While I'm grateful that some people come to Jesus through a "deathbed confession," I'm also saddened by the years they lost outside of Jesus in their one life on earth.

What happens when one believes that the essence of Christianity is getting our eternal destiny secured and that's about it? We come to that transition moment where we enter into a relationship with Jesus Christ and the greatest of transactions takes place. He takes on our sin and we take on His righteousness (2 Cor. 5:21). We're united with Him in baptism (Rom. 6:4). He gets a place on the cross and we get a seat reserved for us at the banquet table in heaven, a "seat in the heavenly realms" (Eph. 2:6). In one sense it's the "rawest deal" of all eternity for Him, and the "ultimate deal" of all eternity for us. Conception in Christ takes place.

Formation, though, is a whole different story. Many believers stop at that milestone moment of transaction with Jesus Christ and think, "That's it! My salvation is secured! That's what Christianity is all about!" There is a place for celebrating the security of our eternal salvation, but this isn't the end of Christianity. It's the beginning. It's a "birth." I've said it before, I'll say it again, and you can say it with me this time: "Jesus didn't just come to bring us eternal life after we die but also to show us how to have a life before we die!"

When we believe that the essence of Christianity is getting our eternal destiny secured and that's about it, we slide into a spiritual holding pattern. Who hasn't been in a spiritual holding pattern? We've settled for baptism, for having our name on the church roll or for that milestone experience with God. Our Christian life can be summed up as pretty much a matter of attending church assemblies on Sunday. After all, we have taken care of our eternal destiny—as though Christianity was some retirement plan in which we enrolled. Retirement—that's a good word to sum up much of our Christian experience after that important transaction. We'll just attend church and live our lives the way we want to live them until the time comes to "cash out" for eternity.

This misconception of the essence of Christianity contributes to generations of people being conceived in Christ and yet abandoning the process of being formed into the image of Christ. This misconception produces countless numbers of church-attenders who are far from Christ-followers. Their spiritual lives are in a holding pattern.

Dallas Willard, a Christian author and philosophy professor at the University of Southern California, calls this kind of Christianity "barcode Christianity."[9] When we go to the grocery store and take our food items to the register, the cashier waves each one over a scanner. Every item we buy has a barcode on it. The scanner's electronic eye reads the barcode. It doesn't respond to anything else on the package. But every once in a while an item will have the wrong barcode on it. Suppose I attempt to purchase a bag of dog food, but the packaging has the bar code for a brand of bread. When the cashier waves the bag of dog food over the scanner the only thing the electronic eye will recognize is the bar code. I may be trying to purchase dog food, but I'll be charged for bread.

Barcode Christianity could sum up many of our lives as believers. We've gone through life wearing our church membership, our baptism or our milestone experience with God as though they were barcodes testifying to our dynamic and ever-growing relationship with the Bread of Life. When asked if we are a Christian, we point to our barcode. And yet our moral lives may be no different from those who don't profess to be Christians. We may be wearing barcodes that say we're "bread," but the truth is our lives are "dog food." We have settled for spiritual conception but have never entered seriously the process of spiritual formation.

What does it mean to move from conception to formation? It means to move from the point of making an intellectual or emotional decision for Jesus and to a lifestyle conversion to Jesus and His instructions for how we should live. It means aggressive effort to see to it that our lives reflect our "barcodes." This is much of what it means to be a disciple of Jesus Christ. Jesus made His desire and intention for every human being explicitly clear when He told His very first followers:

"Therefore go and make disciples of all nations, baptizing them in the name of the Father and of the Son and of the Holy Spirit, and teaching them to obey everything I've commanded you" (Matt. 28:19). Jesus' desire is for all people to become His disciples.

What does He mean by the term "disciple"? In His time a disciple was someone who followed the life and teachings of another person so closely that they became a clone of the teacher. In a teacher/disciple relationship the teacher's goal is not merely to impart information but to enable transformation. The teacher's focus is on developing the disciple into being what the teacher is. Jesus' passion and intention for us is not merely to spiritually conceive us but to transform us into His image, so much so that others would mistake us for Him.

Now you might be thinking, "Come on, Chris, aren't you stretching it a bit? This thing about people actually mistaking us for Him? Is this possible?" According to the Apostle Paul, it is possible: "I always pray with joy...being confident of this, that he who began a good work in you will carry it on to completion until the day of Christ Jesus" (Phil. 1:5-6). God has a passion, a power and a process for moving us from conception to formation.

One of the most difficult things I face in ministry is when a woman experiences a miscarriage. It's impossible for anyone who hasn't had a miscarriage to truly empathize with a woman who has. There is a powerful connection between a woman and the child within her womb, and it's much more than just a physiological connection. It's interesting that the Hebrew word for compassion in the Old Testament (*rahamim*) was derived from the Hebrew word for a mother's womb (*raham*). When the Jews read the Old Testament and came across passages about the compassion of God, it's probable that the image of a pregnant woman and her intense love for the child inside her womb would come to mind.

I can't help but think of this when I consider God's passion for us to move from conception to formation. A miscarriage happens when there's been a conception but the process of formation has been abandoned. Like an expectant mother God longs for us to be fully formed into the image of Christ and is deeply grieved when we abandon this process.

But God won't give up on us as easily as we give up on Him. He's been known to keep pursuing us long after we've stopped pursuing Him. You probably know the story of Peter's denial of Christ. But do you know the words of the angel to the women at the empty tomb on Resurrection morning? "Don't be alarmed...you are looking for Jesus the Nazarene, who was crucified. He has risen! He is not here. See the place where they laid him. But go, tell His disciples and Peter, 'He is going ahead of you into Galilee. There you will see Him, just as He told you'" (Mk. 16:6-7). The angel made it a point to make sure that Peter heard the news and knew that Jesus wanted to see Him as well. Peter may have given up on Jesus, but Jesus hadn't given up on Him.

How about the words of Jesus to the local church in Laodicea? "Here I am! I stand at the door and knock. If anyone hears my voice and opens the door, I will come in and eat with him, and he with me" (Rev. 3:20). This passage is often used in reaching out to people who have not yet made a commitment to Christ. But it is really about Jesus reaching out to believers who've grown "lukewarm" in their commitment to Him. They've experienced conception but have abandoned the process of formation. Though the door to their hearts has, in essence, been slammed in His face, He nevertheless stands and knocks. The sobering news is that often we abort the process of formation. The good news is that He won't abort us.

John Stephen Akhwari represented Tanzania in the 1968 Olympics in Mexico City. He was the last man to finish the Olympic marathon, arriving in the stadium a little more than an hour after the winner. Akhwari had sustained a serious fall while running, and his leg was bloody and bandaged. He completed the marathon wincing with pain at every step. Reporters later asked him why he continued running when he was so far behind everyone else and had no chance of winning. Akhwari replied, "My country did not send me 8,000 miles to start the race. My country sent me eight thousand miles to finish it."

The writers of the New Testament occasionally compared the Christian experience to a race. God didn't send His Son all the way from heaven to earth to be born in a manger, to live a life "with nowhere to lay his head," to die the most gruesome of deaths, and then to arise from the dead, all for the purpose of starting us on the race. God sent His Son so that we could finish it. It's time to move from conception to formation. It's time to move from decision to conversion. It's time for lives that match our barcodes. It's time to recommit ourselves to the process of being transformed into the kind of people who could be mistaken for Jesus. May it be so, Lord. Amen.

Chapter 12

What's in a Name?

Almost immediately after Tara told me she was pregnant we began to discuss names, though we weren't sure whether we were going to have a boy or a girl. Most anyone who's had a baby can recall that privileged agony parents go through in naming their children. After all, names are important aren't they? They usually should "fit" with the last name, although I have to wonder about some people's sense of humor. I went to school with a girl whose first name was Cinnamon. Her last name? Crisp. I kid you not.

But not only should the first name "fit" with the last name, the first name should be one that carries a positive impression. Parents understand this. When was the last time you met somebody named Bathsheba? Or how about Jezebel? Or Judas? Or Lee Harvey? There are certain names that leave distasteful images and memories in their wake.

One morning in 1980 America woke up to the sound of Paul Harvey broadcasting the news that Jimmy Carter, roaring drunk and smashing up everything within reach, had been thrown out of the Moscow Olympics. This, of course, was another Jimmy Carter—a Scottish member of the British swimming team. But can you imagine what Americans thought for a split second when they heard Paul Harvey broadcast a story about "Jimmy Carter" who was the current President of the United States? That same day Harvey went on to report that another Jimmy Carter had been arrested for burglary in Detroit. And he was arrested by a police officer named Richard Nixon.[10]

And I'm not pulling your leg when I tell you this next one. A few years ago a Burger King in the Midwest was robbed. Police arrested—are you ready for this? Burger King was robbed by and police arrested 18-year-old Ronald McDonald.[11]

Now what images come to mind when I tell you these true stories? The irony of Jimmy Carter having the cuffs slapped on him by Richard Nixon? How about a clown being escorted by the police off the premises of his arch rival Burger King? There are certain images so inextricably intertwined with certain names that it's difficult for us ever to separate them.

As you already know, we named our firstborn Skyler. We did so because we found out that Tara was four weeks pregnant just two weeks after she had gone sky diving. That's right, my wife jumped out of a perfectly good airplane at 13,500 feet while she was pregnant (though she didn't know it). We'll pray for her sanity later. We selected Lee as his middle name, though, for a far more significant reason. Exactly one month prior to the day of Skyler's birth, Tara's dad went home to be with Jesus. His middle name was Lee—Douglas Lee McKnight.

Will you let me tell you about him? His story has everything to do with why we gave our little boy some of his name.

Doug was 49 when he died. For 17 years, since the time he was diagnosed at age 32, he struggled with multiple sclerosis. It's a disease of the central nervous system where, for some unknown reason, the body's own immune system attacks healthy tissue. He was at the top of his profession as chief financial officer of a successful oil company in West Texas. Within three weeks of his diagnosis, he was in a wheelchair. The results were incredibly debilitating over the next 17 years and the symptoms were numerous: confinement to a wheelchair, chronic fatigue, urinary tract infections due to the use of a catheter, spasms and tremors in his arms and legs, short-term memory loss, loss of feeling from his fingertips through his toes, blurred vision when trying to read, double vision beyond 50 feet, bouts with depression, poor fine motor skills and insomnia.

Because these symptoms grew in their frequency and intensity in the last few years, Doug was rarely able to feed and dress himself. Only on rare occasions was he ever able to travel to see his children and grandchildren. Nevertheless, in the midst of all his limitations, Doug's passion for and imitation of Jesus Christ shone brightly.

Recently, I read about a four-month refugee Bible class conducted by some missionaries in China. In the class a number of illiterate women had learned to read using the Bible. At the end of four months, the day came when they were to return to their homes. During the final meeting before the women parted, one of them prayed: "We are going home to many who cannot read. So, Lord, make us Bibles, so that those who cannot read the Book can read it in us."[12]

In a similar way, you could read the Book through Doug's life. Certainly Doug was a sinner in need of the cross of Jesus Christ just as much as any of us. He wasn't perfect, but that didn't keep him from trying to emulate the Perfect One. Douglas Lee McKnight, in a body riddled with multiple sclerosis and confined to a wheelchair, left legacies that I hope will live on through his daughter and son-in-law and into the life of his grandson, Skyler Lee. What follows is a sampling of some of those legacies.

A Legacy Of Witnessing

In 1985, three years after contracting MS, Doug initiated and began directing the World Bible School ministry at his home church. The WBS is a ministry offering Bible correspondence courses through which people in countries around the world can learn about Jesus. Under Doug's direction and leadership, the ministry grew to involve as many as 450 volunteers at one time. During his tenure as director of this ministry, people in 20 foreign countries around the world came to know Jesus Christ. More than 89,000 correspondence courses were sent out with almost 2,000 people confessing Jesus as Lord and Savior. With much prayer and careful organization, Doug coordinated this effort from a wheelchair.

Doug didn't just witness around the world, though. He also witnessed in his own little corner of the world. To help him share his faith, Doug wrote out his testimony explaining why he was a Christian and the difference it had made in his life. He then developed it into a letter and concluded the letter with an invitation to visit further about Jesus and the Scriptures. This was Doug's own non-threatening way of sharing his faith, and it allowed people the freedom to respond however and whenever they wanted. It seemed as if he gave this letter to everyone with whom he came in contact—every doctor and nurse that ever attended to him, the pizza delivery people, men at a health club where he would go for exercise in the early stages of his illness, people in his neighborhood, and a multitude of others who crossed paths with him during the course of his life.

Doug's efforts to share his faith bore incredible fruit. Two of the health aides who came to his home to bathe and dress him came to Christ, as well as five handicapped people with whom he came into contact over the course of his illness. He even got to study the Bible with one of the pizza delivery guys. The week before he died Doug received a phone call from a man who had received Doug's letter of testimony some eight years earlier. The man had just read it and was weeping out of conviction and thanksgiving.

From sharing his faith around the world through World Bible School, to sharing his faith in his own little corner of the world, Doug left a legacy that will challenge my son and me in our own witness for Christ. Here was a man confined to a wheelchair for the entirety of his illness and, for the most part, to his house in the last years. Yet almost 2000 people on the other side of the world and seven people in his own little corner of the world confessed Jesus as Lord because of Doug's witness.

Doug did what he could, where he was, with what he had, and it made an eternal difference in the lives of people. Ultimately, I learned through Doug's example that my evangelistic efforts have more to do with my spiritual conviction and courage than my physical condition. Disease may be able to take away a person's body, but it can't take away a person's conviction or message.

A Legacy Of Giving

Shortly after Doug got sick and could no longer work, he became convicted after reading the Bible that he had never put God first when it came to his finances. Perhaps the Scripture that served as the turning point in his attitude was Malachi 3:10 which says that human beings are guilty of robbing God when they neglect to offer Him tithes and offerings. Doug decided that he was going to begin offering to the Lord ten percent of his family's income per month. But he also decided that he wanted to make up for all the years that he hadn't been faithful in honoring the Lord with his income. So he went back in his records to the year that he got his first full-time job and calculated all the money he had made from that point forward. He then calculated what his total tithe would have been for those years had he given ten percent of what he made. Eventually, Doug developed a plan to make up for all those years of not honoring the Lord with his income, and through that plan he gave ten percent of his total income from those years back to the Lord.

Now consider that this was a man whose income dramatically diminished when he got sick, with two teenage daughters, and a wife who had to go to work. Yet he and his family, in essence, doubled their giving to make up for all the years of "robbing God" as Doug would put it.

Doug not only treated God fairly, but he treated others fairly. He loved pizza, and it was a familiar sight for a Pizza Hut delivery car to pull up in front of his house once or twice a week. On one occasion Tara was at the house when his pizza arrived and she noticed that Doug didn't tip the delivery man. She had worked as a waitress for a time at a popular restaurant and was especially sensitive to others in the food service industry, so it wasn't a surprise when she chastised her dad. He decided that she was right so he pulled out his checkbook and assessed all the times he had ordered pizza, calculating how many tips he had neglected to give. Can you imagine the pizza delivery fella's eyes the next time he showed up at Doug's house and received a $50 tip?

Proverbs 11:25 promises that a generous man will prosper, and that he who refreshes others will himself be refreshed. Doug and his family believed that verse and this is why that, though they lived on a diminished income, they were still so generous in their giving. They believed with all their hearts that if they did things God's way then God would provide for them. Years after he got sick, someone gave the family a specially equipped van with an electric wheelchair lift so that Doug could get out of the house and go places. Shortly after his death, Tara's mother, Pam, gave the van away to a family with a handicapped teenager. She could have sold it, but she didn't. Even after his passing, his legacy of giving lived on.

A Legacy of Commitment to a Local Church

If there was anyone who had a viable excuse for not attending Bible classes and worship assemblies on Sundays it was Doug. On Sunday mornings he'd have to get up nearly three hours before Bible class and church began so that the home healthcare aides could get him ready. I think about this often when I consider that there are healthy people all over America who profess to be Christians and yet just can't seem to roll out of bed on Sunday mornings.

A Legacy of Gratitude

A group of people in Doug's church came to him once and said that they wanted to begin praying for him regularly. They asked if he could give them a list of things they could be praying for. The first thing he gave them was a list of 18 things in his life that they could thank God for on his behalf. It was three times as long as the prayer request list he gave them.

Consider what he was thankful for: "my promised eternal salvation, 32 years of disease-free life before stricken with MS, my wife's commitment and devotion to her wedding vows, her strength, her health, her job, Christian friends, only losing one of my five senses, good medical insurance, good doctors, not having contracted something worse." The list went on. Any man in a wheelchair with MS who has a thanksgiving list longer than his prayer request list can teach all of us something about gratitude.

A Legacy of Perseverance

Shortly after being diagnosed with the disease in 1982, Doug attempted suicide. He had driven to the outskirts of Midland, Texas, in the early morning hours with a bottle full of pills and a gun. He parked the car and swallowed all the pills, but thoughts of his wife and daughters and what his suicide would do to them flooded his mind. He managed to make it to a convenience store, called for help and passed out.

Tara's dad never tried to take his life again, though he would endure a gradual and excruciating debilitation over the next 17 years. He had decided that it was God's right—and God's right alone—to determine when he should depart this life. I'm so glad Doug made that decision. For had he succeeded in his attempt, there would be no legacies to write of in this chapter or to live on in the lives of his daughters and grandchildren. By his own admission he made his most significant contributions in life and to the kingdom of God from a wheelchair in a body stricken with MS.

A Legacy of Hope

I wish you could have been at Doug's celebration service. That's what we called his funeral. More than 1800 people gathered to celebrate his life with a slide show, laughter, tears, prayers and the testimonies of several men upon whom Doug left an indelible impression. As I sat in the celebration service, I realized the incredible gift that Doug had given the people who loved him.

He had walked in an intimate relationship with God through Jesus Christ, and because of that he had blessed us in two ways. First, he gave us a legacy of significance, meaning and difference-making to celebrate, and, second, he gave us a future that we could look forward to with eager anticipation. Knowing that Doug was a Christian made all the difference in the world in how we reacted as family and friends to his death. We grieve, and still grieve, for it takes some adjustment for us to get accustomed to life on this earth without Doug. But we also know that we don't have to get permanently accustomed to life without him. For we will see him again because, like Doug, we too are walking with Jesus in this life. That's why none of us told Doug "goodbye" but only "see you later." The greatest gift he gave us was a life that left us a past to celebrate and a future with him to anticipate.

Doug spent the last 17 years of his life in a wheelchair, but when it came to living for Jesus I don't know of many who stood taller or ran faster. Now you can imagine what we think of when we or someone else says "Skyler Lee Seidman." Skyler's middle name will be a rear-view mirror for all of us in the family, reminding us of the legacies his granddad left us to celebrate and incorporate into our own lives. But his name is also a billboard calling our attention to a place in the future where we'll be reunited with his grand-dad once and for all.

So what's in a name? In Skyler's case, everything that matters in life.

Perhaps your name has a story behind it and carries with it positive impressions of a legacy. Maybe you were named for someone special or influential in your family history. Whether or not you were, as a believer you bear a heavenly name. This is what it means to be called a Christian. You wear the name of Christ. Skyler did nothing to earn his granddad's name. We gave it to him in love. The same can be said of your heavenly name. You did nothing to earn it. It was given to you in love.

In Christ's name we have a legacy. It's a legacy of commitment, compassion, love, mercy, obedience, sacrifice and surrender. And it is a legacy that changed the world. In dying He made it possible for us to wear His name. It's a name worth living up to, a legacy worth carrying out. Just as we prayerfully expect that Skyler will live up to his name and carry on his granddad's legacy, so God looks upon us with eager anticipation that we will live up to our name and carry on our Savior's legacy.

Chapter 13

The Emergency Room

Most every parent has to do it. We just got an early start on most parents. It was somewhere around 3 a.m. when Tara and I entered the emergency room. Skyler had been having breathing problems for a couple of days. His little lungs had not been able to take in enough air and the wheezing was growing in frequency and intensity. His breathing rate had grown rapid enough that the 24-hour pediatric physician's hotline recommended that we take him immediately to the hospital for medical attention and observation.

Skyler's cousin, Jake, had some of the same problems when he was Skyler's age. Unfortunately, they had manifested themselves in the form of a frightening seizure late one night. The memory of Jake's daddy calling us early one morning from an emergency room in Tulsa was deeply embedded in my mind. I wanted no part of that terror.

We arrived and Skyler received wonderful care from the emergency room physician. After asking us several questions and making a thorough examination of Skyler, the physician surmised that Skyler probably had asthma (which our pediatrician later affirmed). Those of you who have asthmatic children know what happened to Skyler next—the dreaded breathing treatment.

A medicine called albuterol is poured into a simple contraption called a nebulizer which has oxygen pumping through it. The result is a fine mist which comes out of a tube that is to be held up to the mouth and nose of an asthmatic. As the asthmatic breathes in the mist, the albuterol helps to open up the breathing passages. This breathing treatment can make a remarkable difference in one's capacity to breathe. The problem was that Skyler didn't understand this at all and wanted nothing to do with that strange contraption—especially in a cold, sterile, foreign place such as an emergency room.

After trying everything to coax Skyler into accepting the breathing treatment, I had to resort to more drastic action. I proceeded to press him against my chest, immobilizing his arms, and hold the tube up to his nose and mouth. This was as painful for me as it was frightening and infuriating for him. My heart screamed and squirmed along with his body. I couldn't blame him for his fear, confusion, and frustration. Why would his daddy, who had never hurt him before, suddenly hold him down against his will and continue to cram in his face some dragon with blowing smoke?

This wasn't the first time I had had this experience with Skyler. I vividly remember the time I held him down while the nurse gave him his shots. I'll never forget those eyes—so big and wide out of sheer confusion and terror while his daddy held him down and allowed some lady to stick him repeatedly. He couldn't understand that what I was doing was best for him.

Ironically, his crying and screaming actually worked for him in the emergency room that night because he managed to inhale more of the solution thereby quickening the relief to his breathing passage. The whole ordeal lasted only about ten minutes but it probably seemed like an eternity to him. I know it did to me. Within the hour he was breathing better than he had breathed in days.

That night in the emergency room I got a glimpse of what it might be like from God's perspective when He does what's best for us though we can't see it or don't understand it at the time. He may be the sovereign

Creator of the universe who can see "the end" to which His "means" leads, but that doesn't mean He has ceased to have the heart of a father.

Everyone loves the gentle imagery of God as a shepherd in Psalm 23. But there's a line in that psalm that doesn't sound so gentle. "He makes me lie down in green pastures" (Psalm 23:2). I believe there are times in our lives when God has to make us lie down for our own sake. He has to hold us down for our own good. Like Skyler, we may not always be able to grasp why He's allowing certain things to happen to His child. "'For my thoughts are not your thoughts, neither are your ways my ways,' declares the Lord. 'As the heavens are higher than the earth, so are my ways higher than your ways and my thoughts higher than your thoughts'" (Isa. 55:8-9).

Sometimes God has to take us through the emergency rooms of life in order for us to spiritually breathe again. When God makes us lie down, it is for the sake of nourishing and developing us spiritually. When He holds us down it is always to build us up. When He allows us to be stuck, it is so that we can be strengthened. "And we know that in all things God works for the good of those who love him, who have been called according to His purpose" (Rom. 8:28). From our vantage point, our arms may feel immobilized and there may be some kind of frightening dragon breathing smoke in our face, but the reality is that God has pressed us against His chest. He has us close to His heart. Don't assume that because He knows "the end" that He doesn't suffer with us through "the means." His heart screams and squirms along with us. After all, He is love.

Chapter 14

Daddy's Boy

Skyler is what many would call a "daddy's boy" right now. Why? Because he gravitates toward his daddy. Skyler wants to be with his daddy wherever he is, even at his own risk. Whether his daddy is in the deep end of the swimming pool, the middle of a street or in the pulpit on Sunday morning (which can be every bit as dangerous), my son wants to be where I am and will make an attempt to join me.

But not only does he gravitate toward his daddy, he also seeks to imitate his daddy. Everything daddy does Skyler loves to do. When daddy puts on his shoes, Skyler wants to put on daddy's shoes. When daddy chips golf balls in the back yard, Skyler wants to chip golf balls in the back yard with daddy's clubs.

When daddy wants to eat chips and hot sauce, Skyler wants to eat chips and hot sauce (like I said earlier, even at his own risk). When daddy walks back and forth in the pulpit preaching, Skyler wants to walk back and forth in the pulpit preaching.

More than once it has been said that Skyler is "his father's son." Why do people say that? Because Skyler is constantly seeking to be where his daddy is and do what his daddy is doing. There's nothing more precious and heart-warming in this father's sight than his son wanting to be where his daddy is and do as his daddy does.

The same can be said about how God feels toward us as His children. Nothing makes Him feel more loved and accepted by us than when we want to be with Him and do as He does. "Be imitators of God, therefore, as dearly loved children" (Eph. 5:1). My hope and prayer is that we will live the kind of lives that gravitate toward our Father in heaven as well as imitate Him. In doing so we won't have to tell the world who our Father is. They will know it already because they will see Him in us.

But it is also as sobering as it is heart-warming to see Skyler wanting to be where I am and do what I do. I certainly don't want him to be everywhere that I've been in life and do everything that I've done. I've been places and done things (and sometimes still go places and do things) that wouldn't lead my son to the Father in heaven.

I think of the old story about a father and his young son who were hiking in a dense forest at the base of a mountain range. They came to a place where the hiking was difficult and even dangerous. The father stopped for a moment to get his bearings and consider which way to go. After a few moments of silent thought his son looked up at him and said, "Make sure and choose the good path, Dad; I'm coming right behind you!"

For better or worse our children do come behind us. I often wonder where the path of my life will lead my children. We are a path for our children that either leads to God or away from Him. Ultimately, they will do as they see and not always as they are told.

What will they see in us? Will our lives be an opportunity for them to come to know their Father in heaven? Or will our lives be an obstacle that they will have to overcome in order to know their Father in heaven? Phillips, Craig and Dean, the contemporary Christian music trio, penned the prayerful song that every generation of fathers should be praying: "I want to be just like You because he wants to be like me."[13]

Will you choose the right path with me? They *are* coming behind us.

Notes

1. Ken Gire, *Windows of the Soul* (Grand Rapids: Zondervan, 1996), 44.

2. John Ritter, *USA Today*, September 2, 1999.

3. George Barna, *The Second Coming of the Church* (Nashville: Word, 1998), 2.

4. James S. Hewett, ed., *Illustrations Unlimited* (Wheaton, IL: Tyndale, 1988), 290.

5. Tony Campolo, *It's Friday But Sunday's Comin'* (Waco, TX: Word, 1984), 27).

6. Augustine, in *The HarperCollins Book of Prayer*, compiled by Robert Van de Weyer (New York: HarperCollins, 1993), 43.

7. Craig Brian Larson, ed., *Illustrations for Preaching and Teaching* (Grand Rapids, MI: Baker, 1993), 136.

8. Rich Mullins, "We Are Not as Strong as We Think We Are," *Songs: Rich Mullins* (Reunion, 1996).

9. Dallas Willard, *The Divine Conspiracy: Rediscovering Our Hidden Life in God* (New York: HarperCollins, 1998), 36.

10. Paul Harvey, *For What It's Worth*, ed. Paul Harvey, Jr. (New York: Bantam, 1991), 65.

11. Harvey, *For What It's Worth*, 61.

12. Ken Gire, *Between Heaven and Earth* (San Francisco: HarperSanFrancisco, 1997), 63.

13. Randy Phillips, Shawn Craig and Dan Dean, "I Want to be Just Like You," *Lifeline* (Star Song, 1993).